Literacy through
CREATIVITY

Related Titles of Interest

The Literate Classroom edited by Prue Goodwin
ISBN: 1-85346-566-6

The Articulate Classroom edited by Prue Goodwin
ISBN: 1-85346-703-0

Unlocking Literacy edited by Robert Fisher and Mary Williams
ISBN: 1-85346-652-2

Literacy through
CREATIVITY

Edited by Prue Goodwin

 David Fulton Publishers

David Fulton Publishers
2 Park Square, Milton Park, Abingdon, Oxon OX14 4RN

270 Madison Avenue, New York, NY 10016

First published in Great Britain in 2004 by David Fulton Publishers
Transferred to digital printing

David Fulton Publishers is an imprint of the Taylor & Francis Group, an informa business

Copyright © Prue Goodwin and individual contributors 2004

Note: The right of the author to be identified as the author of this work has been asserted by her in accordance with the Copyright, Designs and Patents Act 1988.

British Library Cataloguing in Publication Data
A catalogue record for this book is available from the British Library.

ISBN 1 84312 087 9

Typeset by FiSH Books, London

Contents

To my father, Jack Penycate CBE, 1913–2003

Acknowledgements

The editor, the contributors and the publisher thank the following for their kind permission to reproduce material used in this book.

Figure 2.1 and 2.2. Used with permission from The Upledger Institute Inc.

Figure 5.1 Photo © Rebecca Sinker

Figure 5.2 Photo © Rebecca Sinker

Figure 5.3 Photo © Rebecca Sinker

Figure 5.4 Photo © Rebecca Sinker

Figures 6.1, 6.2 and 6.3 From *Where The Wild Things Are* by Maurice Sendak, published by Bodley Head/Red Fox. Used by permission of The Random House Group

Figure 6.4 Text and illustrations from *Ginger* by Charlotte Voake © 1997 Charlotte Voake. Reproduced by permission of Walker Books

Figure 6.5 From *Six Dinner Sid* by Inga Moore (1990). Reproduced by permission of Hodder and Stoughton Ltd

Figure 8.1 Screenshot from Sherston's *Naughty Stories* CD-ROM, reproduced with permission of Sherston Software, Malmesbury, Wiltshire

In Chapter 10, extracts from *The Iron Man* by Ted Hughes, published by Faber and Faber

Figure 13.1 From *Clown* by Quentin Blake, published by Jonathan Cape

Contributors

Victoria de Rijke taught primary school children and is currently Principal Lecturer at Middlesex University, London, teaching across Education, Literature and Performing Arts. Co-author and editor of *The Impossibility of Art Education* (1998), *The Nose Book* (2000) and 'The Quack-Project' CD-ROM (2003), she is also on the Children's Literature in Education journal's UK editorial board.

Justine Earl is a Senior Lecturer at Canterbury Christ Church University College teaching on undergraduate, PGCE and further degree courses. She is interested in all aspects of literacy and children's literature, with particular focus on the older, fluent reader in the primary school. She strives to help students and herself make connections across the curriculum and develop creative approaches to teaching.

Wendy Earle is Resources Editor at bfi Education, the British Film Institute. She has worked in educational publishing for nearly 15 years and was previously a Media Resources Officer in ILEA schools. Bfi Education is in the forefront of encouraging the use of moving image media in the promotion of creative learning. She is currently working on an MA in Culture, Media and Communication at the University of London, Institute of Education.

Prue Goodwin taught in primary and middle schools for over 20 years and was an advisory teacher for language development before taking up a post at the University of Reading. Prue edited *The literate classroom*, a collection of articles by leading teacher educators, which was published by David Fulton Publishers in 1999. *The articulate classroom*, a companion volume on speaking and listening, was published in spring 2001.

Judith Graham, although officially retired (and enjoying grandmotherhood), still works occasionally at Roehampton University of Surrey, and she has teaching commitments too in the Faculty of Education in Cambridge. Her interests are in all areas of literacy and children's literature. She is the author of *Pictures on the Page* and *Cracking Good Books* (NATE 1990 and 1997) and co-editor (with Alison Kelly) of *Reading under Control* and *Writing Under Control* (David Fulton Publishers 2000 and 2003, second editions). Her most recent publication (with Fiona Collins) is *Historical Fiction: Capturing the Past* (David Fulton Publishers 2001) which is an edited collection of pieces on historical fiction for children by writers, teachers and academics.

Teresa Grainger is a Principal Lecturer at Canterbury Christ Church University College. Although most of her time is spent in teacher education, she still teaches regularly in classrooms where her particular interests are in the language arts – especially drama, storytelling and children's literature. Her published work includes *Practical Storytelling in the Primary Classroom* (Scholastic 1997), *Resourcing drama 5–8* and *Resourcing drama 8–14* with Mark Cremin (NATE 2000) and *Inclusive educational Practice: Literacy* with Janet Tod (David Fulton Publishers 2000).

Elizabeth Grugeon is Senior Lecturer in English in Primary Education at De Montfort University, Bedford, where she teaches English specialists on the Primary BEd degree course. She is particularly interested in children's literature, language development and oral culture. She is a co-author of *Teaching Speaking and Listening in the Primary School* (David Fulton Publishers 1999) and *The Art of Storytelling for Teachers and Pupils: using stories to develop literacy in Primary Classrooms* (David Fulton Publishers 2000).

Louise Harding is a mature student currently in the fourth year of a BEd degree in Primary Education at De Montfort University, Bedford. Before her return to study she worked as a nursery nurse for 16 years and has a particular interest in Early Years Studies, child development and emergent literacy.

Liz Laycock has been involved in primary education for several decades as a classroom teacher, an advisory teacher and in higher education and ITE. She was Programme Convener for the Primary PGCE and Director of Programmes in the Faculty of Education at Roehampton University of Surrey. She is a contributor to *Reading Under Control, Writing Under Control, The Literate Classroom, Historical Fiction for Children* and *Education in the United Kingdom* all published by David Fulton Publishers. She has also written several books for teachers on aspects of literacy teaching, for Scholastic.

Michael Lockwood taught in schools for eight years before becoming a Lecturer in English and Education at the University of Reading. His publications include *Opportunities for English in the Primary School* (Trentham 1996), *Practical ways to teach standard English and language study, Poetry in and out of the literacy hour* and *Drama in* *and out of the literacy hour* (all three published by the Reading and Language Information Centre, The University of Reading).

Jill Newbald taught in middle and primary schools for 25 years until summer 2003 when she became a School Sports Co-ordinator in Hampshire. Physical Education has always been her specialism and personal interest. As a class teacher she taught the whole curriculum along with her responsibility as to co-ordinator the school's PE programme. In her new role she will be able to focus on developing PE and sport opportunities through a partnership of primary and secondary schools.

Catriona Nicholson was a teacher in primary and special schools before becoming a Lecturer in English and Children's Literature in the Institute of Education at the University of Reading. She has taught on the Reading MA course in Children's Literature and has contributed to various journals and books on the subject.

Margaret Perkins has worked in initial teaching training for many years in different institutions. She previously taught across the primary age range, although is predominantly an early years teacher. Her research has been principally into teachers as readers and the teaching of reading. She has a keen interest in children's ideas about and their response to popular culture.

Angela Pickard is currently a Senior Lecturer in Primary Education at Canterbury Christ Church University College where she works on undergraduate, postgraduate and further degree courses. She lectures in English, Early Years and Physical Education, particularly dance. Her research interests include role play, small group interaction and physical development.

Rebecca Sinker is a freelance artist and educator with ten years' experience researching, teaching, managing and publishing media arts projects across all sectors of education, from primary to postgraduate. From 1998–2003 Rebecca was Research Fellow in Digital Arts Education at the School of Lifelong Learning and Education (LLE), Middlesex University, in conjunction with the Institute of International Visual Arts (inIVA), with responsibility for The Digital Art Resource for Education (DARE – www.dareonline.org).

Ann Whittle began her teaching career in the Caribbean, later returning to Notting Hill as a member of a multiracial, inner city regeneration team. Her priorities have always concerned access to the curriculum for multi-ethnic communities. Now as a freelance trainer and practising CranioSacral Therapist she emphasises the importance of physical nurturing for full cognitive development and the role of the whole body, heart and mind in the learning process. Ann is an External Moderator for a major awarding body in the areas of classroom support and complementary health.

Ruth Wood worked as a primary school teacher for ten years prior to becoming a Senior Lecturer for Information and Communications Technology at Kingston University. She currently works in the areas of initial teacher training and the INSET CPD programme. Although interested in a wide range of aspects related to the integration of ICT within the educational context, Ruth has developed a particular interest in the design and development of multimedia talking books.

Introduction: Creativity and literacy learning

Prue Goodwin

What is creativity?

> Creativity is a prized feature of the human mind, but prizes can coexist with puzzlement. The concept of creativity may trail clouds of glory, but it brings along also a host of controversial questions. The first of these is: *What is it?* (Boden 1994: 1)

Creativity, as discussed in this book, is concerned with how we think, learn, have cognition and understanding of the world around us. It involves ideas, invention, play, resourcefulness, innovation, experimentation, imagination and risk taking. This book does not consider the range of research into 'big' creativity (Feldman *et al.* 1994), through which exceptional individuals significantly change the world as a result of their ideas. It is about what Anna Craft (2001, 2002) calls 'little c creativity':

> ... little c creativity... focuses on the resourcefulness and agency of ordinary people. A 'democratic' notion, in that I propose it can be manifested by anyone (and not just a few), it refers to an ability to route-find, successfully charting new courses through everyday challenges. It is the sort of creativity, or 'agency', which guides route-finding and choices in everyday life. It involves being imaginative, being original/innovative, stepping at times outside of convention, going beyond the obvious, being self-aware of all of this in taking active, conscious, and intentional action in the world.
>
> (Craft 2002: 56)

The contributors to this book consider ways in which the creative process can be harnessed to the advantage of any learner. Any act of creation, invention or experimentation calls on the perpetrator to think, imagine and try out ideas which are new – to that individual if not to the world in general. Each chapter will reflect on how engaging with imaginative and creative activities – such as play, problem solving or artistic invention – enhances learning, specifically literacy learning.

All Our Futures: Creativity, Culture and Education, the report produced by the National Advisory Committee on Creative and Cultural Education (NACCCE 1999) defined creativity as: 'Imaginative activity fashioned so as to produce outcomes that are both original and of value.' The report acknowledges, but does not discuss at length, the use of imagination and invention in the work of everyday learning across the curriculum. Its conclusions, however, relate mainly to the creative arts in the curriculum and in particular to pupils having opportunities 'to produce outcomes that are both original and of value'. Creative activities such as art, music, dance, film-making, drama, design, etc., quite properly have their own curriculum for which end-products will be required. However, a definition of creativity dependent on end-products limits its potential. The NACCCE report has a great deal of valuable comment to make on the importance of creativity and was very welcome at the time it was published because it restored the arts to a central role in the curriculum. However, in primary classrooms teachers need to have a broad view of the place of creativity in their teaching – one that sees it as less about artistic product and more about creative activity being a vehicle to enhance learning.

Jerome Bruner says, 'An act that produces effective surprise – this I shall take as the hallmark of creative enterprise' (Bruner 1962: 18). Creativity is the 'effective surprise' that occurs when unpredictable connections of otherwise unrelated bits of knowledge or experience spark new insights and understanding. This can certainly be brought about through engagement with the arts, but also by grappling with a problem to solve or by searching for the language to articulate an argument. It is the notion of 'effective surprise' that underpins the contents of this volume.

Creativity in the classroom

Generation and appreciation

There are two dimensions to creative activity in the classroom – the generating of ideas and the evaluative judgement of someone else's creative product. Evaluation does not only involve passive appreciation, it can also inspire creative response; for example, writing can be inspired by music or pictures; drama or dance can be stimulated by reading a story or poem. Learners can respond creatively in a wide range of ways. As Eve Bearne (Styles and Bearne 2003: xvii) points out: 'Children now have available to them many forms of text which include sound, voices, intonation, stance, gesture, movement, as well as print and image.' Pupils are familiar with both creating and interpreting multimodal texts, as well as working on artistic interpretations of their ideas. Essentially it is the engagement of the imagination that will determine the breadth and depth of an experience, and the consequent learning. As Ted Hughes (1988: 36) says: '... imagination, with its delicate wiring of perceptions, is our most valuable piece of practical equipment. It is the control panel for everything we think and do, so it ought to be education's first concern.'

Vulnerability and curiosity

Young children need little or no encouragement to use their imaginations and to be creative. Babies play with language when they first start to imitate sounds (Weir 1962) and Kornei Chukosvsky (1965) records the 'topsy turvies' of word play so adored by toddlers. Their natural curiosity and readiness to experiment allows them to wallow in language. Their 'mistakes' are positive steps towards the linguistic conventions of their communities. Three-year-old Johnny, for example, demonstrated his growing confidence to use past tenses when he declared, 'Me wented to Grandad's' and to invent new words based on logical use of his developing vocabulary with 'Mummy, it's beezing hot'. No one would criticise Johnny or suggest that he had failed in some way – on the contrary, he is applauded for his resourcefulness.

As with language, so with other forms of representation. At the Foundation Stage there are seldom children who are thrown by being asked to draw their meanings, or to sing or move in response to their 'work'. Their curiosity about how things sound and feel far outweighs any concern about whether they look foolish or who might have been the 'best'. However, as they get older, some children become less willing to engage in creative activities and it is not unusual for both children and adults to announce that they can't draw, sing or act. Where does this insecurity come from? It appears to relate to a fear of failure, or at least concern about an unfavourable comparison with the products of others. If the product of creativity is under scrutiny, of course, we become very vulnerable; people feel insecure when they believe they are being judged. Many teachers feel reluctant to be creative in the classroom because their own experiences of the arts involved the assessment of a product. Maybe comparisons were made between end-products such as paintings or they were made to 'perform' in front of others. In this book, creativity is not linked to a product-outcome. Art, drama, dance, music and invention – although recognised as important aspects of childhood experience in their own right – are considered here as vehicles to support literacy.

Creativity in the literacy lesson

Inspiring children to write or asking them to respond to literature through the creative arts (art, music, drama or dance) offers a range of learning opportunities to all. Exploring and questioning a text can extend and challenge convention. Having the opportunity to express an understanding of text in a variety of ways supports all pupils, in particular those with dispositions towards visual, auditory or kinaesthetic learning. Take, for example, the following sessions with two classes of eight-year-olds. The first session was in preparation for writing based on the story of Beowulf; the second was in response to the story *The Great Piratical Rumbustification* by Margaret Mahy.

Story, sights and sounds

The story of Beowulf's battle with the monster, Grendel, was told in a dramatic fashion. Following the storytelling, the children discussed which bits had been scary and how they would have behaved if they had been attacked by Grendel. The children used facial expressions and mimed positions of fear or attack. What sounds might they have heard? They made sounds with whatever came to hand – voices for the yells of battle, rattling wall-bars for the clang of weapons and selected musical instruments for more specifically focused sounds. Back at their tables, the children drew quick sketches of the battle and of Grendel as they imagined him to look. As they worked they talked about how the battle took place in firelight (so there would be flickering shadows), about the blood splattered walls of the hall and the bellows of both monster and warriors. All the storytelling, listening, talking, moving, acting, artwork and music making took less than an hour. The resulting written work was full of effective description and lively vocabulary. Drama, music, art and dance took place during the session but not with any intention to perform – purely to help the effectiveness of the writing. The engagement of all the senses in interpreting different parts of the story offered visual, auditory and kinaesthetic support to all the children – especially those for whom language and literacy are not easy. A collection of published versions of the story (in particular by Heaney (1999), Patten (1999) and Crossley-Holland (1999) were available for further reading and literacy work.

Finding a solution

The story *The Great Piratical Rumbustification* by Margaret Mahy (1981) is rich in ideas and language that was explored through a variety of creative activities. For example, the invention and problem solving that took place when the class discussed how to produce an invitation to a pirate party. The only information they had from the book was that: 'The sign of a pirate party is a message in the sky – the words "Pirate Party", written over the stars.' In groups of four the children discussed how the message could have got into the sky. Among the many other ideas they came up with, particularly notable were the formation flying parrots and the message being spelled out by the souls of dead pirates transformed into stars.

FIGURE 1 Invitations to a Pirate Party: parrots and pirate 'souls'

Government documents

Although there has always been support for creativity in the National Curriculum (NC) and National Literacy Strategy (NLS) documents, it has not been highlighted as prominently as, for example, planning or assessment. But now creativity as a means of learning is making a comeback and teachers are being encouraged to see both innovative thinking and the use of the creative arts as means to achieve the learning objectives for literacy.

The NC recognises that imaginations are triggered by having problems to solve, tasks to complete or ideas to discuss and these can be generated through creative activity such as drama, music or art.

The words 'respond imaginatively' have been present in the NC for English since the Cox Report (1987), however, it wasn't until 1999 that imaginative response was exemplified. 'Children should respond imaginatively in different ways to what they read, drawing on the whole text and other reading – for example, using the characters from a story in drama, writing poems based on ones they read, showing their understanding through art or music' (DfEE 1999: 47).

With the coming of the NLS in 1998, many primary teachers felt discouraged from using creative approaches in their literacy lessons. However, from the start, although easily overlooked within the plethora of folders and videos produced by the NLS, creative approaches of some kind have been promoted. For example, in an NLS document downloadable from the internet entitled 'Strategies to enhance children's understanding of texts' (see Websites in References section) we find advice about:

Constructing images (visualising, drawing, drama)

- Creating visual images is claimed to improve comprehension by linking prior experiences to the new idea thus building richer schemas
- During and after reading children can sketch what they see, undertake freeze frames of key moments in a story and make models based on the text

Character development

- Imagining how a character might feel; identifying with a character, charting the development of a character over time in a longer text
- Hot seating
- TV interviews
- Drawing characters

and in a set of fliers supporting a range of writing experiences (DfES 2001) there are many references to the centrality of interacting with story in all its forms:

Writing narrative – principles

- The roots of story writing lie in a rich experience of listening to and watching stories, drama and role play, early story reading, frequent rereadings of favourites and the telling/retelling of all forms of story.
- Use drama, video and puppets to help build up the content and context for stories.

(NLS Writing Flier 2, 2001)

Although the NLS can appear functional and didactic, since its outset, the use of imaginative approaches has been included and more recent advice puts far greater emphasis on creative response and stimulation – especially through drama.

It is pleasing to see that creative approaches to teaching literacy are not only being suggested but actively advocated by the Qualifications and Curriculum Authority through *Creativity: Find it, promote it* (see www.ncaction.org.uk) and by the Primary National Strategy through its document *Excellence and enjoyment* (DfES 2003) which has set out a far more flexible agenda than primary schools have seen for 15 years. Excellence and enjoyment includes the statements: 'Promoting creativity is a powerful way of engaging pupils with their learning' (DfES 2003: 34) and 'We want all schools to be creative and innovative in how they teach and run the school' (DfES 2003: 43). However, proclaiming the need for creativity and innovation cannot ensure that all primary teachers – especially those who qualified during the last ten years – feel competent to carry it through. It is the intention of this book to offer all colleagues some starting points for being more creative in their classrooms.

An intention to support

This collection of articles aims to draw together a wide variety of thoughts on how creative approaches assist pupils who are learning to read and write. The contributors, all of whom are involved in literacy education, range in their style of writing from the academic to the anecdotal. The contents of each contribution encompass research findings, theoretical underpinnings, case studies and straightforward practical activities. The linking factors between the chapters are:

- the supremacy of story (told, read, re-enacted, drawn, written, watched, heard, etc.)
- the conviction that opportunities for children to call on every aspect of their own creativity, on the creativity of others (particularly through the creative arts) and the creativity of their teachers, will enhance and support their literacy learning.

In her chapter, Liz Laycock reflects on *All our futures* (NACCCE 1999) and the major role it is playing in reinstating the importance of the creative arts in the primary curriculum. Laycock sets out the political context for a revival of practices which have been recognised in schools for decades. However, this book is not just about reinstating the value of well-established methods. It also advocates that teachers embrace both the broad range of artistic endeavour, incorporating film, computer texts and multimodal representation alongside the more traditional, and the sort of curiosity that triggers innovative thinking and problem solving. The contributors advise building on the best of the old whilst welcoming the challenges offered by new and constantly changing technologies.

Body, brain and literacy learning

Ann Whittle considers the latest research into the cognitive processes of the brain and she highlights the physical and cognitive needs of all learners. Since Gardner's ground breaking work into multiple intelligences (Gardner 1983, 1993), work on different learning styles and the development of accelerated learning practices advocated by Carla Hannaford (1995) and others, there has been a far greater recognition of the need to cater for a variety of learning styles. Multisensory learning, making use of each appropriate sense when tackling new ideas, encourages teachers and learners to engage their visual, auditory and kinaesthetic modes of understanding. An ability to relate to others and to reflect on one's own learning both enhance the quality and depth of what is being learned. In her chapter, Ann Whittle provides a description of how the brain operates, the need for physical movement and the engagement of the senses when learning. Using dance, drama or music as vehicles for literacy learning may be an alternative or supportive approach for some pupils, for others they may be the most direct or only route to understanding.

Stories and language play

By considering the content of young children's fantasy stories and their own imaginative games we are surely forced to wonder about the general inadequacy of a principle that claims that our knowledge of the world and experience accumulates gradually from the known to the unknown.

(Egan 1988: 13)

Elizabeth Grugeon and Louise Harding's chapter on playground language and Margaret Perkins' on popular culture, remind us that children are naturally creative when left to their own devices or when encouraged to explore the texts within their peer group culture, such as comics and superhero cards. Rebecca Sinker and Victoria de Rijke also concentrate on the language of childhood. They describe work carried out with children in London primary schools and the development of two CD-ROMs which feature language, play, visual arts and music. The integration of play, drawing, voices and the work of artists and composers bring children into a wholly creative situation – trying out ideas and inventing for themselves whilst surrounded by the creations of others.

Creative readers

Judith Graham (Chapter 6) and Catriona Nicholson (Chapter 7) illustrate the ways young readers become the makers of meaning through their interaction with every aspect of a book. Graham and Nicholson show that having time to look, to read, to think and to talk allows children to become reflective, critical and discriminating readers. Ruth Wood considers how well, or otherwise, the act of reading transfers to the computer screen. Wood expresses concern that information technology, potentially the most exciting source of innovation, has so far produced rather uninspiring 'talking books' and she looks to a future when the full potential of information technology will allow children to be equally creative as readers of page or screen.

Ways into writing

In her chapter, Teresa Granger describes the powerful support that drama can provide for young writers who may be struggling with that most complex task – composition. Grainger demonstrates how becoming part of a story (be it through an original improvisation or one based around a book) enables children to find their own voices so that when they come to write, they literally have something to 'say'. Michael Lockwood observes the writing of poetry in an urban middle school. Lockwood follows the process from initial inspiration through to a finished piece of writing and comments on the ways children are supported to extend their vocabularies or use more adventurous phraseology.

The dancing page

The poet Benjamin Zephania tells us that: 'The rhythm of the pen goes bubbling, dancing across the page' (Zephania 1990) and, in considering the links between the PE curriculum and literacy, Jill Newbald and Prue Goodwin see dance as a major contributor to children's exploration of texts. Angela Pickard and Justine Earl pick up on the dance theme, taking it further in terms of the literacies of music and movement and the many parallels to be made with literary study.

Looking at literacy

Chapter 13 considers visual literacy and the role played by art, particularly drawing, in children's interpretation and creation of meaning. Moving image, especially film and television, inevitably form a large part of children's narrative experience. Children's implicit recognition of this is demonstrated in Chapter 13 while Wendy Earle, in Chapter 14, explains how the British Film Institute is encouraging teachers to use film to inspire many aspects of literacy work in the primary school.

Conclusion

Tom, the most successful learner of all

In his book *How Tom beat Captain Najork and his hired sportsmen*, Russell Hoban offers a most persuasive argument for letting children learn through creative exploration and problem solving. Tom spends his time 'fooling around', much to the disgust of his iron-hatted aunt, Miss Fidget Wonkham-Strong. She sends for Captain Najork who 'teaches fooling around boys the lesson they so badly need'. This book directly challenges the value of sticking too rigidly to imposed systems and structures. Tom represents free-flow creative play, which can appear confused and messy and which has no apparent product. There are no finishing posts for fooling around, no winners or losers and no specialist equipment. The Captain and his sportsmen are the personification of an authority that demands regulation, instruction and competition. Training rather than teaching. It is because Tom had engaged creatively with his environment that he had developed the necessary skills to beat Captain Najork and the hired sportsmen at their own games.

Creative teachers

If we were being literal and pedantic, it could be argued that Tom needed a little bit of structured learning (after all, even the most liberal minded teacher would find 'fooling around with dustbins, with bent nails and with broken glass' slightly dangerous; the health and safety committee would have field day!). However, it is the responsibility of every primary teacher to seek out the most creative ways to teach and to model the culturally curious learner. Practitioners concerned that they themselves lack creativity should remember the assertion that 'it exists in every individual and awaits only the proper conditions to be released and expressed (Rogers 1954). Teachers who choose to ignore the potency of creative approaches need to consider what they and their classes will miss in terms of powerful learning experiences. A didactic, highly controlled piece of teaching may be far easier to plan and to quantify in terms of outcome but it is unlikely to have the lasting effect of a creative encounter with literacy.

It is not necessary for teachers to be skilled as actors, musicians or dancers to successfully include creative arts in their literacy lessons. Nor do they need to prepare complex explorations or experiments to encourage the sort of creative thinking that children use when problem solving. In an address to a conference 'Creating conditions for creativity' held at the Institute of Education, University of London in June 2003, John Barrett, from the Department of Experimental Psychology at the University of Bristol, listed regular features of successful creative classrooms. The list indicated that in creative classrooms, teachers and learners:

- relax and enjoy their learning
- are curious and questioning
- encourage and support effort
- are intrinsically motivated, persistent and spurred on by challenge.

All it takes to provide the conditions for creativity in the classroom is for teachers to be open minded, flexible and prepared to take a few risks. The greatest risk is the commitment of time. Time to allow children's minds to wander through a variety of possibilities; time to do the necessary focused day-dreaming that every author does; time to comprehend, and then present, abstract thoughts through practical activity; and, time to engage the imagination in whatever literacy task is undertaken. It will not be time wasted.

Creativity can be uncomfortable, unpredictable, anarchic, boundary breaking and insecure but it is also playful, invigorating and pleasurable. It has been the cause of all great leaps forward in humanity's understanding of the world and a stimulus of the small steps that we all take as we learn. As Jerome Bruner says, in the gender bound language of the early 1960s:

> There is something antic about creating, although the enterprise be serious. And there is a matching antic spirit that goes with writing about it, for if ever there were a silent process it is the creative one. Antic and serious and silent. Yet there is good reason to inquire about creativity, a reason beyond practicality, for practicality is not a reason but a justification after the fact. The reason is the ancient search of the humanist for the excellence of man: the next creative act may bring man to a new dignity.   (Bruner 1962: 17)

References

Boden, M. A. (1994) *Dimensions of creativity*. Cambridge, Mass.: MIT Press.

Bruner, J. S. (1962) *On knowing: essays for the left hand*. Cambridge, Mass.: Harvard University Press.

Chukosvsky, K. (1965) *From two to five* (translated by Miriam Morton). Berkeley and Los Angeles, Calif.: University of California Press.

Craft, A. (2001) 'Little c creativity' in Craft, A., Jeffrey, B. and Leibling, M. *Creativity in education*. London: Continuum.

Craft, A. (2002) *Creativity and Early Years Education*. London: Continuum.

Crossley-Holland, K. (1999) *Beowulf*. Oxford: Oxford University Press.

DES (1989) *Report of the English Working Party 5–16* (The Cox Report). London: HMSO.

DfEE (1999) *The National Curriculum: handbook for primary teachers*. London: DfEE.

DfES (2001) *NLS Writing Flier 2: Writing narrative*. London: DfES.

DfES (2003) *Excellence and enjoyment*. London: DfES.

Egan, K. (1988) *Teaching as storytelling*. London: Routledge.

Feldman, D. H., Csikszentmihalyi, M. and Gardner, H. (1994) *Changing the world*. Westport, Conn.: Praeger.

Gardner, H. (1983) *Frames of mind: The theory of multiple intelligences*. London: Heinemann.

Gardner, H. (1993) *Multiple intelligences: The theory in practice*. New York: Basic Books.

Hannaford, C. (1995) *Smart moves: Why learning is not all in your head*. Atlanta, Ga.: Great Ocean.

Heaney, S. (1999) *Beowulf: a new translation*. London: Faber & Faber.

Hoban, R. and Blake, Q. (1974) *How Tom beat Captain Najork and his hired sportsmen*. London: Jonathan Cape.

Hughes, T. (1988) 'Myth and education' in Egan, K. and Nadaner, D. (1988) *Imagination & education*, pp. 30–44. Milton Keynes: Open University Press.

Mahy, M. (1981) *The Great Piratical Rumbustification and The Librarian and the Robbers*. London: Puffin.

National Advisory Committee on Creative and Cultural Education (1999) *All Our Futures: Creativity, Culture and Education*. London: DfEE.

Patten, B. (1999) *Beowulf and the monster*. London: Scholastic Children's Books.

Rogers, C. R (1954) 'Towards a Theory of Creativity', *ETC: A Review of General Semantics*, 11, 140.

Styles, M. and Bearne, E. (eds) *Art, narrative and childhood*. Stoke-on-Trent: Trentham Books.

Weir, R. H. (1962) *Language of the Crib*. The Hague: Mouton.

Zephanaia, B. (1990) Extracts from 'Pen Rhythm' in Styles, M. and Cook, H. *Ink-Slinger*, p. 13 London: A&C Black.

Websites

'Strategies to enhance children's understanding of texts' (NLS 2000) can be found on www.qca.org.uk

Creativity: Find it, promote it (see www.ncaction.org.uk)

Chapter 1

The arts and literacy in primary classrooms

Liz Laycock

In 1999 the appearance of *All Our Futures: Creativity, Culture and Education*, the report from the National Advisory Committee on Creative and Cultural Education (NACCCE) was greeted by those who knew of it (for it was not circulated to all schools!) with relief and delight. Mike Newby, Chair of the Universities Council for the Education of Teachers, told the committee:

> 'How exciting it was to read this report. It isn't often that a document of this kind can stir in me the kinds of feelings this one did – a desire, mainly, to stand on my chair and cheer – but yours hit the spot. At last some fresh thinking about the future, carrying with it the authority of not one but two Secretaries of State.'

As an educator who believes in a truly 'broad and balanced' curriculum in primary schools, I was one who shared this delight. If this report were to inform a revision of the National Curriculum, perhaps we could begin to move away from the rigid subject boundaries, the overemphasis on literacy and numeracy to the detriment and often neglect of the 'less important' foundation subjects, and the overwhelming prescription which was suffocating teachers' creativity and imagination. Unfortunately, by the time the committee reported, the revised National Curriculum (1999) was ready so the recommendations were not reflected in the revisions and appeared, until recently, to have sunk without trace.

All Our Futures identifies economic, technological, social and personal challenges which need to be addressed by education, and suggests that we need 'to develop active forms of learning which engage young people's creative energies' (Rogers 2000, p. 4). The report argues that 'there are important relationships between creative and cultural education, and significant implications for methods of teaching and assessment, the balance of the school curriculum and for partnerships between school and the wider world' (NACCCE 1999, p. 6). In developing five main themes, the members of the committee consider the challenge to education in establishing new priorities, 'including a much stronger emphasis on creative and cultural education and a new balance in teaching and in the curriculum'. They believe that all people have creative abilities, that these are different for all of us and that when we find our creative strengths 'it can have an enormous impact on self-esteem and on overall achievement' (p. 7). They stress that they are not advocating an undisciplined 'free for all'; the encouragement of greater creativity in education requires 'a balance between teaching skills and understanding and promoting the freedom to innovate and take risks' (p. 10). Alongside and related to creative development is the need to foster cultural under-standing: 'Education must enable [pupils] to understand and respect different cultural values and traditions and the processes of cultural change and development' (p. 7).

The NACCCE, in this report, emphasises that creativity is not confined to the Arts but is to be found and nurtured in the whole curriculum: 'One of our aims in this report is to emphasise the importance of the arts and their essential place in creative development. But creativity is not unique to the arts. It is equally fundamental to advances in the sciences, mathematics, technology, in politics, business and in all areas of everyday life' (p. 27). Nevertheless, there is particular concern that aspects of the Arts and humanities are being neglected because 'the curriculum is already over-full' (p. 14). The conventional academic curriculum, as it is taught in many schools, does not generally encourage the development of pupils' social, spiritual and emotional needs nor does it encourage ques-tioning, experimentation or originality, all of which are essential to nurturing creativity. The curriculum, as it stands, defines a body of knowledge which is to be 'delivered' to learners. Although it is possible to make links across subject boundaries and to create learning contexts which make sense to pupils, most schools are so preoccupied by the need to cover the prescribed ground that such links have barely been explored. There are schools and teachers who have sustained a balanced curriculum, who have fostered the Arts and humanities and have shown that this can also enable pupils to achieve high levels of literacy and numeracy. In a recent (2002) Ofsted survey of successful primary schools the Chief Inspector identified important factors in their success; they tailored the curriculum to the needs of their own pupils and they were flexible but clear about learn-ing objectives and approaches to teaching. 'There was also a strong emphasis on enquiry, problem-solving and practical work such as taking part in live theatre, because the head-teachers knew that these were powerful ways to engage pupils in learning' (Bell 2002).

Such approaches are likely to allow pupils to demonstrate achievement which is different from that identified in strictly academic contexts. *All Our Futures* also argues that creative and cultural education are relevant and necessary in contributing to rais-ing academic standards:

> Every child has capabilities beyond the traditionally academic. Children with high academic ability may have other strengths that are often neglected. Children who struggle with academic work can have outstanding abilities in other areas. Equally, creative and cultural education of the sort we propose can also help to raise academic standards. The key is to find what children are good at. Self confidence and self esteem then tend to rise and overall performance to improve. High standards in creative achievement require just as much rigour as traditional academic work. (p. 13)

Primary teachers, who teach all aspects of the curriculum to their classes, are ideally placed to provide contexts in which all pupils can flourish because 'subjects' do not need to be taught separately. They are generally aware of their pupils' differing learning styles and areas of strength and, given the freedom to do so, can plan both content and teaching approaches which meet the needs of individuals. Teachers know that 'intelligence is multifaceted' (Gardner 1993) and that children are not necessarily 'less able' because they do not perform well in the academic tasks related to words and numbers (reading, writing and numeracy) so valued in schools. A broad curriculum which includes opportunities for all children to work at what they are 'good at' is essential, especially at the primary level when the skills foundation is laid. Teachers need to maintain confidence in their own professionalism and understanding of how children learn and be prepared to take risks. Such teachers are generally imaginative and creative themselves and set out to provide activities which draw on children's existing knowledge and experiences and which are interesting. They have clear aims for what they hope children will learn and also have high expectations of the children's achievement.

> 'Creative teachers . . . need techniques that stimulate curiosity and raise self esteem and confidence. They must recognise when encouragement is needed and confidence threatened. They must balance structured learning with opportunities for self-direction and the management of groups with attention to individuals. They must judge the kinds of questions appropriate to different purposes and the kinds of solutions it is appropriate to expect.'
> (*All Our Futures*, p. 95)

In classrooms with teachers like this, there is generally a lot of talk, not just from the teacher, but by children who are working collaboratively, discussing problems and sharing ideas both with each other and with the teacher. Children are given time to pursue interests and ideas; they may sometimes take a whole day to work on a project or theme. There may often be self-directed, exploratory play with materials and resources such as musical instruments, computer programs, clay, paint, or textiles – what author Philip Pullman, in a recent speech to graduates at Roehampton University of Surrey, termed 'fooling about' – to enable children to explore the qualities and potential of material they are working with, as well as their own hypotheses and ideas, without heavy direction from the teacher. These classrooms will reflect Britain's rich cultural and linguistic diversity, celebrating the variety of story and literature, art and music around them and demonstrating that the cultural experiences and traditions of all children are valued.

The English and Literacy curriculum in these classrooms is lively and imaginative. Teachers' knowledge of and enthusiasm for children's literature is at the heart of the teaching. Their wide knowledge of a range of literature enables them to select texts which provide real contexts for teaching aspects of the literacy curriculum, where 'connections between text, sentence and word level knowledge (are made) explicit to children' (*Effective Teachers of Literacy*, (see Medwell and Wray), p. 2). One such teacher commented in an article in the *Times Educational Supplement* (Brown 2003), that the use of *The Wreck of the Zanzibar* (Michael Morpurgo) as the basis for several weeks' work with a Year 5 class not only covered the NLS framework for this year group but also 'stimulated cross-curricular topics and discussions'.

> From turtles to self sufficiency, sibling rivalry to worship, there was hardly an area of the primary curriculum that it did not touch upon. We found it almost indecently easy to cover all the remaining objectives in the literacy framework for Y5 term 3, but with not an extract in sight.
>
> (Brown 2003)

The Programme of Study for English in the National Curriculum (1999) states that, at Key Stage 1, 'pupils should be taught to respond imaginatively in different ways to what they read' and, at Key Stage 2, in addition to this, they should 'evaluate ideas and themes that broaden perspectives and extend thinking'. In order to meet these requirements there must be links to other areas of the curriculum such as art and design and music, as well as much talk and discussion. Other chapters in this book demonstrate clearly the ways in which children can 'respond imaginatively' to literature through art, music and dance. Aidan Chambers (1991, 1993), among others, has shown the ways in which children's thinking and understanding of, sometimes challenging, themes in texts can be developed through discussion. An element of guided reading sessions in the literacy hour, especially at Key Stage 2, should be discussion about what is being read, with opportunities for children to express responses to events and characters, to articulate what they have inferred from the text and to listen to and perhaps disagree with others' interpretations.

Understanding and response can be developed even more fully in drama sessions. A recent research project by the Centre for Literacy in Primary Education, written up as *The Reader in the Writer: The links between the study of literature and writing development at Key Stage 2* (Barrs and Cork 2001), documents the use of drama both as preparation for reading texts and as a means of developing children's understanding and ideas before they begin writing. Whilst the texts themselves and the approaches used to teach writing were clearly major factors in enabling children to produce high quality writing, the use of drama with the children was a further contribution to their success. Susanna Steele and Fiona Collins, who led the drama sessions with the children, commented:

> 'Working with drama prior to reading a text can develop an engagement with the characters and events that can inform, sustain and enrich children's commitment both to investigating the language, form and structure of the text and their subsequent writing. Drama offers an interactive way of working that enables children to use their own knowledge, understanding and experience in conjunction with the events in the narrative. The emphasis is on collaborative work using individual, group and whole class strategies that enable children to bring their understanding to the text initially in an active rather than discursive way.'

Inspired by this work, Year 2 teacher, Gabriella Wraight, decided to investigate the potential of such an approach with younger children. Among other books, she used *The Tunnel* (Anthony Browne) as a book which offered, in both text and illustration, possibilities for discussion and a context the children could explore through drama. Browne's work frequently conveys more to readers through the illustration than does the written text and children often perceive more than adult readers of the issues addressed. This was certainly true of these children. Having explored the relationship between brother and sister in their drama, they were able to write very effectively in role as one of the characters, successfully sustaining the first-person narrative stance, as this example shows (the child's spelling is unaltered):

The story of Rose

My name is Rose. My brother Jack dose not get along with me. It started off when me and my brother were arguing and mum told us off. She replied 'go out and think about your behavey-our.' So we went to the wast ground. It had lots of rubish on the floor. And my brother said 'why did you have to follow me?' I said 'its not my fult we are in this arful place.' Jack went to exsplor. And behind the bushis was a tunnel. 'Hey' said Jack. 'There is a tunnel'. He went in the tunnel. I was scerd but I had to save my brother even when he was being nasty to me. I went in the tunnel. The tunnel was sticky, slimy and dark. At the end of the tunnel was a wood. It was quiet. Suddenly the wood turned into a forest. I ran as farst as I could. I ran like the wind because I was scerd. At the end of the forest I saw my brother still as a pile of stone. And I huged him and cried and he turnd back to normule. He said 'I knew you would come'. We went throght the woods then the tunnel and the wastground and back home. My mum was seting the table. She said if everything was alright. I smiled at Jack and he smiled back to me. I felt happy because my brother didn't get heurt.

Having the opportunity to discuss their writing with both the teacher, in writing conferences, and each other, as writing partners, as it proceeded also contributed to the quality of the writing. Many of the children involved had not been confident writers before this change of approach. Over several months both confidence and achievement increased because of the constant discussion and feedback from the teacher, as well as their work in drama.

More creative and imaginative approaches to teaching both reading and writing require rigorous monitoring by the teacher, so that teaching can be adapted in the light of children's progress and needs. Formative assessment, with constant feedback directly related to the tasks in hand, is essential if children are to be fully engaged in their own learning and progress. *All Our Futures* addresses issues relating to standards and assessment and they affirm that 'Methods of assessment must be appropriate to different types of learning if they are to encourage and not inhibit the creative and cultural development of young people' (p. 107). At present, the emphasis is on summative assessment of 'measurable outcomes'; 'such testing tends to concentrate on testing pupils' recall of factual knowledge and skills which can be measured comparatively. It generally takes little account of experimentation, original thinking and innovation ... Some areas of the curriculum, especially arts and humanities; some forms of teaching and learning, including questioning, exploring and debating, and some aspects of particular subjects are neglected' (p. 109).

Teachers' understanding of the distinction between 'assessment *of* learning' (summative) and assessment *for* learning' (formative) has been much enhanced by the work of Black and Wiliam and the research teams at King's College, London, and the Assessment Reform Group at Cambridge University, in recent years. If we take seriously the need to sustain children's confidence in themselves as learners, the principles articulated in these studies need to be the basis for ongoing assessment. *All Our Futures* summarises these:

- it must be built into the design of the teaching programme as an integral element, rather than added on to it;
- pupils should be actively involved in the processes of assessment and contribute to them;
- it must be focused on the development of each individual: i.e. it must be criterion referenced rather than norm referenced;
- the evidence it provides must be acted on if teaching is to be tuned to the range of pupils' individual developments. (p. 113)

Observation of the process of carrying out a task, of the strategies a child is using and the mistakes he or she is making is often more important than the final product which may not reflect the thought which has taken place. Effective teachers of literacy monitor progress in this way; they are 'making use of well developed systems for monitoring children's progress and needs in literacy and using the resulting information to plan future teaching' (*Effective Teachers of Literacy: Summary* p. 2).

A further aspect of the recommendations in *All Our Futures* is not yet widely implemented. Teachers generally need to make much greater use of the expertise of those outside the classroom and the contribution this can make to children's creative and cultural education.

> The work of schools can be supported by a wide network of other partners and providers, including community groups, business, industry and cultural organisations. By 'cultural organisations' we mean museums of all kinds – for the arts, sciences and humanities – galleries, performing arts organisations, sports organisations and other subject-based or youth organisations ... This sector includes artist-in residence schemes, children's theatre, theatre in education, education liaison programmes of major cultural organisations and community-led projects which are based in the arts and cultural activities. (p. 120)

Some schools make regular use of storytellers, performance poets, dancers and musicians for events such as book weeks or cultural events, drawing on members of the local community, but longer term involvement of artists or writers in residence is much less common in individual schools. Where this does happen and children are given time to work on substantial projects, they show real interest and commitment, learning much from experts and producing high quality work. An example of children working with an artist is given in the Ofsted report, *Expecting the unexpected* (2003). This was a Year 4 art project which covered learning objectives in science, English, history, as well as art and design.

> Having learned about the form, pattern and symbolism of Tudor portraits pupils visited the National Portrait Gallery with the teacher and resident etcher. Pupils recognised many of the paintings and were amazed at their small size. They sketched the figures and examples of the background patterns. Back at school, given a small sheet of copper they developed their designs to that size. They covered every stage of the process guided by the artist. The highlight was a visit to the artist's studio to use her printing press where they experienced the thrill of seeing their designs unfold. The project lasted a whole week. (*Expecting the unexpected*, p. 12)

Several museums and galleries are keen to establish strong partnerships with schools. As well as 'bringing many cultural voices into the gallery, including poets, storytellers, puppeteers and illustrators to work alongside artists and art historians' (Grigg 2003) with children, the Tate Gallery, led by Colin Grigg, ran a three year project (1999–2001) in collaboration with the Institute of Education, London University, called Visual Paths to Literacy. The project worked with ten primary schools. 'A forum, comprised of teachers from participating schools, decided the themes and approaches of each term's work, ensuring activities were relevant to their children's needs and the demands of the National Curriculum and the National Literacy Strategy . . . A freelance team of writers provided gallery workshops, undertook school placements and teacher in-service on the chosen themes' (p. 129) There were also writers in residence each year (Grace Nichols, Michael Morpurgo and Anthony Browne). The children's writing produced as a result of their involvement on this project was sensitive, perceptive and of high quality. Many of the children involved used English as an additional language. 'For these children, visual images provided a powerful bridge between the different cultures and languages' (p. 131). Projects such as this demonstrate the potential of such partnerships and there are moves to increase them in different areas of the country – see the Creative Partnerships website. There are even suggestions, coming from gallery education departments and the TTA, that the experience of trainee teachers could be widened by their carrying out some school experience in a museum or gallery setting.

If this were to happen, newly qualified teachers would enter the profession well prepared to encourage new partnerships with other creative groups outside schools. In recent months there has been a greater thrust towards promoting more flexibility in curriculum planning and delivery, especially in primary schools. Ofsted is keen to demonstrate what successful schools are doing and to show that those who teach a broad curriculum, with considerable time allocated to the arts and humanities and links made across subject boundaries, do achieve good results in the formally assessed areas of literacy and numeracy. The QCA has established a web-based resource with examples of creative teaching projects and there is a further set of examples on the Arts Alive website. Hopefully teachers will have the confidence to trust their professional judgement, take a few risks, and allow their own creativity and imagination to inform approaches to teaching.

Acknowledgement

I should like to thank Gabriella Wraight for allowing me to include an example of her children's writing.

References

Assessment Reform Group (1999) 'Assessment for Learning' in *Assessment for Learning Beyond the Black Box*. Cambridge: University of Cambridge School of Education.

Barrs, M. and Cork, V. (2001) *The Reader in the Writer*. London: Centre for Literacy in Primary Education/London Borough of Southwark.

Black, P. and Wiliam, D. (1998) *Inside the Black Box*. London: King's College School of Education.

Brown, S. (2003) 'Forget the objectives, bring back some joy', *Times Educational Supplement*, 23 May.

Browne, A. (1989) *The Tunnel*. London: Julia MacRae Books.

Chambers, A. (1991) *The Reading Environment*. Stroud: Thimble Press.

Chambers, A. (1993) *Tell Me: Children, Reading and Talk*. Stroud: Thimble Press.

Gardner, H. (1993) *Frames of Mind: The Theory of Multiple Intelligences*, 2nd edn. London: Fontana Press.

Grigg, C. (2003) 'The Painted Word: Literacy through Art' in Styles, M. and Bearne, E. *Art, Narrative and Childhood*, Chapter 11. Stoke-on-Trent: Trentham Books.

Medwell, J. and Wray, D. (nd) *Effective Teachers of Literacy: Summary of Findings*. London: Teacher Training Agency.

National Advisory Committee on Creative and Cultural Education (1999) *All Our Futures: Creativity, Culture and Education*. London: DfEE.

National Curriculum Handbook for Primary Teachers (1999). London: DfEE.

Ofsted (2002) *The Curriculum in Successful Primary Schools*. London: Ofsted.

Ofsted (2003) *Expecting the unexpected*. London: Ofsted.

QCA (2003) *Creativity: Find It, Promote It*. London: QCA.

Rogers, R. (ed.) (2000) *All Our Futures: A Summary*. London: National Campaign for the Arts.

Websites
Creative Partnerships www.creative-partnerships.com/
www.ncaction.org.uk/creativity
www.ncaction.org.uk/artsalive

Chapter 2

The body of learning: the eight senses in literacy and creativity

Ann Whittle

The body as a tool-kit

The body is the ultimate tool-kit for learning. One could say that learning is what the body does best. It takes in information second by millisecond, sends it to central controls like the pons, thalamus and amygdala in the heart of the brain where it is sorted for factual content and emotional significance before making its appropriate onward journey.

The body is the great information gatherer with storage facilities and processing plants beyond our conscious imaginings. It has a nervous system which can all at once collect and perceive the subtlest nuance of change on a person's face, process and evaluate this on an emotional Richter Scale and respond appropriately through a continuum of the subtlest of body language and sound to the clearest of actions.

It will keep us safe from danger through the fight or flight response of the reticular alarm system and the adrenal glands. It will provide the calming conditions to heal wounded tissue and recycle damaged cells, digest and assimilate nutrients, keep our biological rhythms stable and allow us to sleep.

In short this body-consciousness is an amazing biological and energetic computer in which the files do not have to be opened because, except in accident or illness, they are never closed. Even under full anesthetic or in coma it is thought that parts of the limbic system of the brain remain awake to watch and monitor.

We are often led to believe that the focus of learning, language and creativity is monopolised by the part of the body we call the brain and that this is somehow distinct and separate from the rest of the body – an autonomous organism in its own right. There is no doubt that the brain is phenomenal. Professor Vilayanur Ramachandran delivering the Radio Four Reith lectures (Ramachandran 2003: 1) states that the brain: 'is the most complexly organised structure in the Universe . . . made up of one hundred billion nerve cells or neurons . . . Each neuron makes something like a thousand to ten thousand contacts with other neurons and these points of contact called synapses are where exchange of information occurs.' He goes on to say that the number of 'brain states', i.e. the number of possible permutations and combinations of brain activity, exceeds the number of elementary particles in the known universe.

What is important to us as educators is how we access this structure. We may be in awe of the brain's complexity within itself but the often forgotten miracle is in its links to the rest of the body through the motor/sensory and autonomic nervous systems together with its interface with the rest of the world through the senses. The senses are 'the front of house staff' in this body of learning. There is no other way in.

There are many current scientific models of how the body accesses and stores information in the form which we call 'learning' and which we recognise as such in the development of skills like reading and writing. In this chapter about the senses we are going to refer to just three of them.

The first is the traditional scientific/medical model which sees the brain essentially as the master organ of the human body and almost distinct from it. In this model these bundles of nerve fibres alone are perceived as the seat of our mental and emotional life, our feelings and our sense of self. This is the model where research is directed into detailed study of brain tissue and function and how the brain makes links between what are perceived as discrete and separate structures.

The second is 'The Triune Model of the Brain' developed by Dr Paul MacLean (cited in Hannaford 1995), where he distinguishes three stages of evolutionary development within the brain and names the areas in terms of age and function as reptilian, early mammalian and neo-mammalian. He clarifies through this model that although we have a 'human' neo-cortex as part of our brains, all stages of our evolution are represented in that organ and ignored at our peril if we are to fully understand our 'human' behaviours. The philosophy behind this model is that the foetal brain develops through the evolutionary stages of our forebears to its current limitless potential at birth and beyond.

Our senses and their pathways through the body are very old in evolutionary terms. Most sensory stimuli come into the brain stem, pons and medulla oblongata (see Figure 2.1) situated deep in the skull just above the spinal cord and named by MacLean in his Triune Model as the reptilian brain. As we evolved into Homo sapiens we kept all aspects of our previous evolution, such as a fight and flight mechanism and survival strategies which make us hungry and drive us to shelter.

In time we developed viviparous birth and mammary glands to nurture our young in infancy and emotional ties and loyalties formed us into families and tribes. This phase is represented by the limbic system comprising the thalamus, hypothalamus, basal ganglia, amygdala and hippocampus (see Figure 2.2). The work of Joseph LeDoux (cited in Goleman 1996) indicates that the limbic system is not just a set of organs or structures but a series of emotional circuits which interlink at key junctures and are absolutely integral in learning and behaviour.

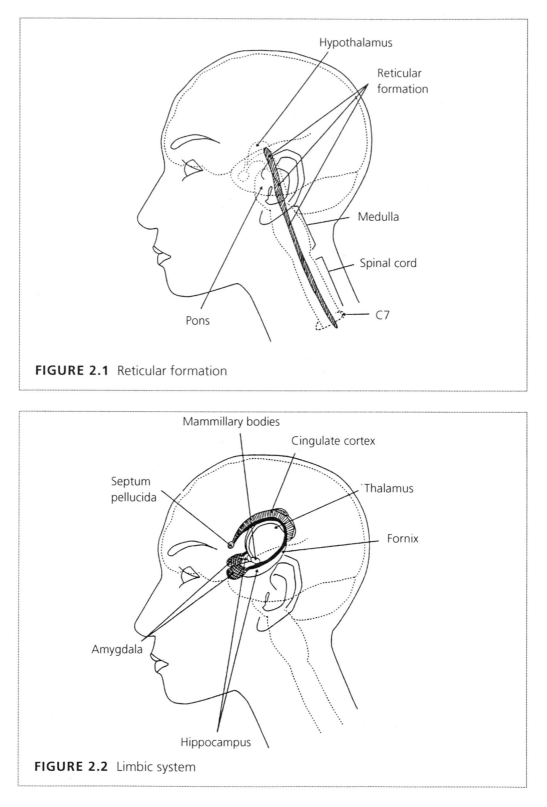

FIGURE 2.1 Reticular formation

FIGURE 2.2 Limbic system

The thalamus acts as a relay station between all incoming senses (except smell) and the cerebral cortex, also relaying motor impulses from the cerebral cortex through the brain stem and out through the muscles. In this way all information coming in is attributed with an emotional charge, positive or negative or maybe only boredom. We transform that raw *emotion* as educators into *moti*vation and use it to great advantage.

The largest part of the brain is the cerebrum. It is covered by the neocortex, a thin layer of 'little grey cells', 2 to 5mm thick, of which Monsieur Poirot was so proud! Although the neocortex comprises only one quarter of the brain's volume it has 85 per cent of the total neurons (Hannaford 1995: 71). These neurons have unlimited ability to organise and reorganise neural pathways from new experiences throughout life. The left and right halves of the cerebral cortex are what we usually think of as our 'brain'. Formed as four main lobes they are joined by a most important structure called the corpus callosum. This facilitates the cross-over connections between sensory perception from the right side of the body to the left cerebral hemisphere and the left sided sensory input to the right hemisphere. Now in our evolution we can begin to develop language and self-expression, master rational thought and identify and evaluate our preferences, motivations and ambition.

From this model it is easy to see how it is natural for us to learn through a sequence of sensation, emotion and rational thought. Indeed it always feels natural for us as teachers in any presentation of new information, to begin with sensory stimulus. Along with this comes the emotional/motivational charge to encourage participation and finally the intellectual reasoning or explanation needed to complete the task.

The third model of learning which is useful for us comes from quantum physics and sees the entire brain and body-consciousness as an energy field not limited to the extent of the physical body which we normally see and feel. In this model we are inextricably linked to other beings and the whole of creation and the extent of our creativity as an individual is to the degree to which we are able to tap into the universal energy field or Zero Point Field, becoming known now as just 'The Field' (McTaggart 2001) which holds all the information there ever was or ever will be. The brain in this model is like a radio, a receiving set and the extent to which we have the ability to 'attune' is a mark of the information we can access and the memory we can activate. Although the terminology of this model is modern it actually embodies the principles of ancient healing arts which have been known for thousands of years in China, India and among indigenous peoples.

This model explains the adage that 'there is nothing as powerful as an idea whose time has come'. It may illumine how inventions like the telephone or scientific knowledge manifests in different parts of the world without apparent prior communication. Jung's concept of a collective unconscious is now accepted as commonplace. We know that children often have great understanding and inspirations beyond our adult minds and if we are wise we may acknowledge these with great benefit to their self-esteem and development.

All three of these models serve our purpose as educators because each one has a gift of understanding for us and each one uses the same radio-tuning mechanisms to gain access to and evaluate the environment that impinges upon us as individuals. These tuning mechanisms we call the senses.

The eight senses

These are: vestibular/proprioception, hearing, touch, smell, taste, sight, intuition and knowing. They are of course traditionally considered to be five in number: the senses of hearing, sight, touch, taste and smell. However recent research suggests that the most delicate of our sensory systems, which monitors our relationship and connection to the earth, our sense of balance, motion and equilibrium begins to form in the embryo about three weeks after conception. By five months in utero it is fully developed and ready for use. This is the vestibular system and sense of proprioception. I refer to it as the zero sense. Sensitive and complex, lying in the mastoid bone behind the ear lobe the vestibular system includes the utricle, saccule, semicircular canals, and vestibular nuclei of the medulla and pons. The vestibular nuclei are like a bundle of neurons carrying impulses from the semicircular canals and cerebellum to the Reticular Activating system (RAS) in the brain stem (Figure 2.1). The RAS transmits these impulses to the neocortex alerting it to incoming sensory stimuli. Carla Hannaford clearly explains this process in her book *Smart moves* (p. 35):

> This 'wake up' by the RAS gets us ready to take in and respond to our environment and to learn. This connection between the vestibular system and neocortex as well as the eyes and core muscles is highly important to the learning process.

This means that in order to learn, the body has to move, so the increasing determination of educators to re-establish a physically and creatively dynamic curriculum is exactly on track to support our children.

Next to form is the organ of hearing and this by seven months after conception so that the foetus is able to hear and identify phonemes and language even before birth. It would seem that we are naturally predisposed for language learning and full entry into the language environment. The biologist, Rupert Sheldrake (1999) describes this great flowering of speech and linguistic propensity in the young child as attributable to morphic resonance 'through the collective memory on which individuals draw... it should in general be easier to learn what others have learned before'. Morphic resonance greatly enhances the capacity which even toddlers develop to generate and use language which they have never actually heard.

Now, in the newborn, the kinesthetic senses of smell, taste and touch, become crucially important at birth and in the bonding process. Add to this an important aspect of the zero sense, proprioception; the body's sense of itself in space and the sense of deep touch. Deep in the tissues are receptors which monitor the degree of stretch in our muscles and feed back to us everything we need to know about our physical position. Hugging, caressing, closeness in baby carriers and ancient practices such as wrapping in swaddling clothes and foot bandaging are all cultural manifestations of this need of the tissues in young babies to feel themselves and their boundaries. Later it will manifest in skateboarding, theme park rides and mountain biking pursuits where skills of balance and boundaries become highly honed in the young adult.

So the sense of proprioception defines for us our position in space in relation to the earth and manifests for us our understanding of gravity. The head needs movement in order to learn. Nothing switches off the brain more effectively than watching television or driving on the M6 motorway.

The sense of proprioception extends through all the musculature and is essential to our sense of where we are in space and our relationship to earth. We underemphasise the importance of this learning at our peril, for the body is where we live and we cannot learn except in our bodies any more than we can use computer software that has not been loaded.

Finally, of the physical senses, sight begins to develop. How we process and utilise the sense of sight is complex indeed. Professor Ramachandran observes that: 'we primates are highly visual creatures and it turns out that we have not just one visual area, the visual cortex, but thirty areas in the back of our brains which enable us to see, perceive the world' (Ramachandran 2003: 2). Some scientists now believe that the brain processes new visual information 'through holographic transformation of wave interference patterns' (McTaggart 2001: 95). It appears that when we see things, we are reading information from the Zero Point Field on a quantum level, and our brains use this information to create the images (holograms) which we see in front of us and at the correct distance from our bodies. What is so fascinating for us as teachers in all this dynamic creative research is that whichever model we relate to, the accessing mechanisms are still the eyes and the physical sense of sight.

Lastly to the senses of intuition and knowing which are particularly strong in young children. Some scientists believe these to be higher cognitive processes and not based in the physical body. However we find in ancient cultures many references to intuition as a 'third eye' and the solar plexus as 'the seat of the soul'.

In the part of the autonomic nervous system which is in charge of biological balance we find bundles of nerves (plexi) that act as 'little brains' and these are especially focused and powerful at the waist and in the sacral/abdominal area. Dr John Upledger (1996) refers to these plexi as 'the abdominal brain', in colloquial language we know them as 'gut feelings'. Our knowing sense will defy logic and against all the facts will sometimes say: 'Hold it! There is something else here that I know and I need to bring into consciousness before I act.'

Sensory learning styles

Much information is now available concerning the ways we access the environment around us through our senses and our preferred accessing styles. So we speak now of visual, auditory, kinesthetic learning styles as commonplace. Some people who use all their senses to build their model of reality then need time and space to step back momentarily to process the information before giving a response. We may refer to this style as digital. Most people mix and match with several styles but often under stress one or two will tend to dominate.

Visual learners usually have good spacial awareness and like to work with charts, graphs, pictures and maps. They like neat surroundings, have an eye for colour and style and in their speech will use visually related language, e.g. 'do you see what I mean? 'I get the picture!' Physiologically they will hold their body upright and often when questioned will find the answer on the ceiling or out of the window!

Auditory learners may talk a great deal, love music, songs, stories and reading aloud. They will be tuned in to voice tone and tempo, volume and rhythm. They may be good at languages and be good mimics. They could well favour the language of sounds: wavelength, harmony, resonate, clash, tune and chatter. They will hear the answer to the question in their inner ear so may turn their head to find it and will offer their dominant ear to the teacher's voice.

Kinesthetic-tactile learners want to touch, to feel, to manipulate objects and often to suck their pencil! Physical movement is important to them as they are sensitive to their own body's feelings and sensations like the clothes on their skin and the chair on which they are sitting. Physiologically they often work in a flexed (bent) position so that they can access their abdominal brains in the solar plexus because for them that is where the answer is. They work from their 'knowing sense' and will speak in measured tones because saying exactly what they mean is important. Through their words they are sharing their feelings, so they may not be first to put up their hands and may shy from self-disclosure.

Digital learners like rational clear explanations and enough time to do the task. They like to know the rules and follow them. They do not necessarily work well in groups as they like to go at their own pace and have peace in which to think. They often relate well to non-sensory words such as think, explain, understand, remember and recognise. They tend to find the answer by logically working it out and will only be satisfied when they can perceive the whole process through to the result.

How we take in information is very likely to be the way we offer it to others so it important for us as teachers to know our own learning style and to vary the teaching styles we use. However we build our model of the world, we have to do it through using our sensory perception, intuition and knowing. There is no other way for inter-action and learning to take place. By offering all four learning styles in a teaching session we provide 'a treat' and 'a challenge' to each pupil, thus ensuring that essential motivation and delight in the learning process.

The needs of the body

The whole body and brain are used in learning and the more strongly we and our children are rooted in our bodies and aware of our eight senses the more safely and surely we will progress. The body is our most precious resource and that it has needs cannot be overemphasised.

It needs water to keep the electrical circuits of the neural pathways sharp and clean. It needs water to make sufficient cerebro-spinal fluid to bathe the brain and spinal cord, bringing nutrients in and taking waste away to be excreted through the venous system.

It needs nourishment to provide the precious trace elements for the immense neurological processing required for a successful day in the classroom and a strong and robust immune system to make new stem cells and nerve cells, to recycle and repair damage to strained or broken tissue and to produce all the myriad of fighting force, cells and molecules, which keep infection at bay.

Finally it needs periods of rest. The body cannot maintain stimulation all the time. The parasympathetic nervous system which is responsible for the involuntary and healing mechanisms such as digestion, assimilation, breathing, circulation and excretion does not work so well when we are constantly under stress. The need to return to homeostasis or biological balance is very strong and very necessary: time to play, time to sleep, time to dream – and time to be a child.

References

Hannaford, C. (1995) *Smart Moves: Why learning is not all in your head.* Atlanta, Ga.: Great Ocean Publishers.

Goleman, D. (1996) *Emotional Intelligence.* London: Bloomsbury.

McTaggart, L. (2001) *The Field.* London: Harper Collins.

Ramachandran, V. 2003 BBC Radio Four Reith lectures. Lecture One: Phantoms in the Brain; Lecture Two: Synapses and the Self.

Sheldrake, R. (1999) *Dogs who Know when their Owners Are Coming Home.* London: Hutchinson.

Upledger, J. (1996) *The Brain Speaks Study Guide.* Palm Beach, Fla.: The Upledger Institute Inc.

Chapter 3

Discovering creativity on the playground

Elizabeth Grugeon and
Louise Harding

> Creativity is ordinary, normal: it is the everyday process of semiotic work as meaning-making.
>
> (Kress 2003: 40)

We don't know the extent of children's creative thinking unless we listen to them and closely observe what they are doing. People such as Michael Armstrong (1997), Iona Opie (1994), Vivien Paley (1984) and Carolyn Steedman (1985), among many others, have done this and opened up a world of child meaning-making and understanding. For some time now trainee teachers at De Montfort University (DMU) have been encouraged to observe what children are doing on the playground, to talk to them and find out about their play. They have discovered that the playground is a richly intertextual and creative site where children play out narratives of their own devising.

Observing play

This chapter begins with Louise's research at breaktime and her own attempts to make meaning of what the children are doing on the playground when they are largely free of adult jurisdiction. In the spring of 2003, Louise observed a group of Year R (ages 4–5) on their small rural school playground. She writes, 'I observed a group of five children assemble in a large corner. After a brief huddle they all joined hands, one girl crouched down on her haunches and began to bounce along whilst another pulled fiercely in the opposite direction. As I watched, Emma joined me and I asked her if she knew what the group was playing. "Mums and Dads," she replied, "I can tell, that's what they always play and I'm a little sister called Gracie." Emma then ran off to join the group that was now moving vigorously round the corner. On closer observation I could hear Polly using a shrill type of American accent to shout, "Naughty dog! Naughty dog!" she proceeded to chase the "dog" as it/she ran in circles, barking loudly. At this point "baby" began to cry and Polly stopped running to comfort her with, "Okay daaarling, it's aaalright". "Naughty dog" kept running in smaller circles whilst "baby" was attended to by "mummy" and "sisters". Polly shouted, "that's it, we're off!" and the group reassembled in a huddle in the corner, leaving the "dog" on her own. She then drifted slowly over to the group whining loudly and crouched down next to "baby".'

Louise continues to comment on this episode: 'This appeared to be a well rehearsed and organised episode with a very definite plot, range of characters and their associated dialogue and body language . . . This group of girls could be seen practising and re-enacting a familial scene with all its implications for exploring the language of relationships, hierarchies, behaviour and self esteem. Role play such as this can be interpreted as an important life rehearsal; young children will act out the experiences that are meaningful to them and try to make sense of those that can be confusing and powerful.' Kitson cites Erikson (1965) who

> stresses the importance of the life rehearsal element in fantasy play, suggesting that, through play children can begin to learn to cope with life and with a range of complex social issues...
> (Moyles 1994: 92)

It is evident that this role play is also providing an opportunity for the children to become involved in narrative.' Louise suggests that 'whilst playing, children are "storying" (Whitehead 1997) the events and actually verbalising their sequence, whether through characters and dialogue, actions, or a running commentary. Whitehead suggests that "narrative is the spoken or written account that tells about the story's events. Narrative is thus essentially a 'telling'" (1997: 99).' Louise felt that this emphasised the importance of oral storytelling since these children seemed to be using it so successfully to organise and explore their own experience and she refers again to Whitehead's suggestion that 'the ability to place ourselves right in the centre of a story is a valuable start to becoming a reader and writer' (1997: 94). It seemed to her that, 'the intricacies of the children's role play stories enacted on the playground could be seen as the beginnings of this'.

Having watched the girls, Louise later turned her attention to a group of five boys as they moved rapidly round the playground, providing more evidence of the spontaneous creativity of their rather different narratives. She writes, 'They clustered, broke away, grabbed each other and regrouped, talking over each other loudly.' It soon became obvious to Louise that the content of their play was changing as quickly as their movement. When asked, one explained, 'The Indians are the baddies, we have to shoot the baddies. Power Rangers have red, yellow and blue' – but the game seemed to fall apart in disagreement until another boy arrived waving his arms like wings. This was evidently an invitation to play and 'the whole group suddenly began running and a game of chase began with one boy shouting, "Suck your blood! Suck your blood!" Two girls who had previously been "babies" joined in and I watched them pretend to die/faint when caught by the "vampires" and then become "vampires" themselves. At times it was hard to decide whether the victims were being rescued or transformed, but

I did notice that the "vampires" were particularly gentle with the "babies"!' This notion of gender awareness is illustrated by Vivien Paley's observation of children's play: she writes,

> Should a monster (always a boy) chase them, he must follow girls' rules: no forceful capturing. The boys are willing to accommodate the eccentricities of girls but expect other boys to understand the need for rough play. (Paley 1984: 20)

Louise felt that this example of vigorous and imaginative play was shaped by the children's familiarity with video and television, particularly *Buffy the Vampire Slayer* and *Power Rangers*. The children had told her that they watched these on Cartoon Network. She had heard a lively discussion in the classroom about 'transformers' and a 'super hero robot' and had noticed that children brought these toys to use on the playground. She writes, 'The youngest boy in the class was very interested in "Super Hero" and this was often reflected in his animated conversation, drawing and emergent writing and "small world" play in the sand.' She considers the fact that adults may question the suitability of the wide range of programmes on video and TV that young children are watching but feels that there are positive advantages and cites Naima Browne's argument that television and videos can provide significant support to young . . .

> writers' development, not through providing lessons, explicit or implicit, in the physical aspects of writing but rather through providing children with a rich experience of stories told in different ways to different audiences and also an experience of different genres. (Browne 1999: 107).

It seemed to Louise that, 'many story lines of fantasy games can be compared to the genre of more traditional tales of heroes and monsters and good triumphing over bad'. In their play she had observed children using a range of complicated dialogue and 'alien' vocabulary demanding careful pronunciation. 'Young children's memory and acute attention to detail amaze me when it comes to their verbal and pictorial description of favourite characters in programmes and films. All these emerging skills are a result of engaging with a media form that excites interest and fires the imagination of the children. They identify with and become their "super heroes" and although play may often appear rough it is important as an adult to look more closely at the level of speaking and listening involved, the storytelling organisation of events, development of character and intrinsic understanding of plot.'

Creative play and 'cultural capital'

Louise recalls how 'as a member of staff in a nursery school it was policy to discourage the children from playing games like *Power Rangers* and *Karate Kid* and any "fighting" games which used props and improvised construction toys that could be substituted as weapons. This meant that adults often intervened and altered what was potentially a high level of imaginative play.' She reflects, 'perhaps if we had observed before stopping their activities we may have recognised parallels with the emerging literacy development being fostered in the classroom' and quotes Marsh and Millard (2000) who suggest that 'Because contemporary children's play is often bound up with popular cultural icons which are unfamiliar to many adults, suspicion is cast as to its inherent value' (p. 45). Louise feels that if teachers of young children are prepared to recognise what children already know and can do (what Marsh and Millard call their 'cultural capital') and acknowledge that this will include their considerable exposure to media and popular culture outside school it can be used positively in the classroom. She refers to *Curriculum Guidance for The Foundation Stage*:

> Young children's learning is not compartmentalised. They learn when they make connections between experiences and ideas that are related to any aspects of life in the school setting, at home and in the community.   (DfEE 2000: 45)

She concludes her observations by suggesting that it would 'seem developmentally appropriate to capitalise on the wealth of language and literacy displayed on the playground, use the children's interest in and understanding of popular culture and their creative involvement in role play and bring this into the classroom as a basis for teaching literacy'.

In this reflective account of her close observation of the children she is teaching, Louise is herself engaging in highly creative meaning-making, striving to make sense of what she has seen and heard and to relate it to her own knowledge and understanding as an emerging teacher. Her detailed observations and commentary have been echoed in the experiences of other trainees working with 4- to 11-year-olds on playgrounds. They have illustrated Marsh's assertion that

> Children engage in a semiotic world in which texts in different modes are conceptually linked. They do not see a neat dichotomy between print and televisual texts as they move seamlessly from one mode to another in their quest for meaning-making...they use visual, literate, oral and corporeal modes of communication in a range of multimodal practices.   (Marsh 2003: 43)

Discovering the power of pretending

Noreen was fascinated by a version of the chasing game 'it' 'where the children substituted their real selves for Disney characters. The only male in the threesome was Captain Hook while the other two players played Sleeping Beauty and Belle.' She comments, 'Here three characters from popular children's animated films were being used in this game. The girls played helpless females being chased and captured by Captain Hook...Another group consisted of three boys playing "hospital", using *Holby City* and *Casualty* as a guide. Their role play titles were "Doctor", "Poorly Person" and "Ambulance Person"... the Ambulance and Doctor ran madly round the playground to offer assistance to the Poorly Person. The wooden playhouse was now a hospital, the bench inside used as a bed. The dialogue was sophisticated, "Yes, it's the doctor speaking. Can I help you?" To which the Ambulance Person replied, "We got a Poorly Person here. Help!" ' (March 2003).

In an urban lower school in 2001, Susan described the way children were using collectable soft toys in their play:

> Many children were involved in games based on *Pokémon, Bouncing Bone Heads* and *Beanie Babies*... they were not necessarily playing with the objects but using them as a stimulus to develop very involved drama based games requiring discussion, collaboration, negotiating and listening.

She watched three six-year-old girls:

> ...one had Mystic, the unicorn *Beanie Baby,* and for most of the game, it hung out of her coat pocket while the following activity was carried out. All three girls leapt out of the school door and wove their way around the playground flapping their arms. I later found out that these were their wings. They finally met up in a grassy area of the playground well away from the school buildings. They gathered leaves, twigs and grass from the nature area and arranged them in little piles.

In conversation with her, they described how they were making little nests; this was clearly intertextual reference to *The Lion, the Witch and the Wardrobe,* as they told her, 'our teacher read us the bit about the fawn who lived in the forest'; and also, she thought, to *Bambi* – they were all familiar with the Disney video. As they played, she overheard their discussion, 'unicorns don't lay eggs, they have babies'. However, they agreed to eggs and collected food for the expectant unicorn.

Imaginations at work

Looking at what the trainee teachers have recorded shows the extent to which children from 4- to 11-years-old creatively absorb experiences from inside and outside school in their play culture – exploring themes and issues that they make their own through imaginative narratives. Looking at what the children tell trainees shows the extent to which influences from TV and film, Harry Potter, Pokémon, Beyblades, far from deadening their imagination, feed and extend possibilities for new narratives.

In March 2002, Clare interviewed three Year 4 boys:

Child 1	Well, we get our ideas from Card Captors and Pokémon...me and Jacob had the idea of using transporters – like little machines, walking transfers.
Child 2	Transport us in the worlds...
Child 1	...bringing the future into the world of dragons and back into the present – into our normal world...

Child 3	. . . and magical world.
Clare	What is it called?
All	Dragon Cards.

Listening to them, Clare realised that these 'cards' are entirely imaginary. She writes: 'They go on to describe how they fire arrows through the cards which unleash the dragons and allow them to battle with them.' She feels that they have drawn upon a range of media influences here:

> Card games such as *Pokémon* and *Card Captors* have inspired Child 1 to come up with a game that has similarities to those games mentioned, but with his own imaginative input. They have produced imaginary cards of dragons with varying powers. The three children all know what the different cards are and what they do, without having to actually see them. They have given the dragon cards names such as 'Ghost Dragon', 'Thunder Dragon' and 'Ice Dragon'. These represent the elements and what the children might class as dangerous things. The idea of magical worlds comes from their different media experiences; the words they use clearly reflect these. Included in their game is a city called 'Diagon City' which has been taken from *Harry Potter*. Another of their interests was the TV programme, *Dungeons and Dragons*. Their game includes weapons, guardians and creatures of power.

Interestingly, all these are constituent parts of the archetypal myths which have underpinned fantasy fiction from the oral tradition to *Star Wars*.

The children continued to talk to Clare:

Clare	Do you have any accessories, bits you need to play the game?
Child 1	Well, we need the cards.
Child 2	The stick that we use to fly on and we use to shoot the animals.
Child 1	. . . and me and Jacob and John have just started a story . . .
Child 3	. . . the Fairy Dragon.
Child 1	No, Ice Dragon – our first ever card is the Fairy Dragon and our second card . . . is the Ghost Dragon.
Clare	Do you buy the cards?
Child 1	No, we pretend we have them.
Clare	Oh, do you make them up?
All	Yes.
Child 1	We find them – we can't capture the champion levels, which are Ice Dragon, Fire Dragon or Lightning Dragon, because they are more powerful than any card – so we have made up cards – mine's the Ghost Card.
Child 3	Mine's the Demon Card.
Clare	Do you have those? Do you draw them out or do you pretend you have got them?
Child 1	We pretend we've got them.

Looking at this long discussion, the imaginative involvement of these three boys in their game is impressive:

Clare   And you made the whole thing up yourselves?

Child 3   Yep, with a few ideas from other things.

This kind of heightened involvement is illustrated by examples the trainees have collected and which they frequently comment on. Natasha writes:

> Most prevalent on the playground were 'pretend' games. They varied between those that used stories and characters obviously derived from popular media and those that involved more of the children's own imaginative construction. The children were extremely keen and able to describe the narratives of their games; they appeared to be very intense. There were many games that were directly based on stories or themes taken from the media such as *Harry Potter*, *Buffy the Vampire Slayer*, *Blind Date* and *Pop Idol*.

Many of the games required the players to have considerable knowledge to enable them to construct games. Carla saw children playing 'a narrative game based on ideas from the Disney and Pixar film, *Monsters Inc.*' (2002). She felt that in order to create this game, the children needed to have a 'sound knowledge and understanding of the characters, setting and plot to make it into their own version'. She also noticed that 'when playing the game, the children were able to demonstrate clear comparisons between the good and bad monsters through their use of language and actions':

Child B   You have sharp teeth and claws.

Child C   Yeah, like Randall. I like being him; he's nasty and cheats and changes colour.

Lorraine had been reading Tyrell's (2001) *The Power of Fantasy in Early Learning*: 'Children need places to hide ... not all children want to dash about or kick a ball around' and recognised this on her own playground, 'the field allowed the children to vary their play. The field is a very large open space with lots of trees and bushes on the edges. These areas provided large spaces for children to make dens and turn these areas into imaginary spaces. I saw these areas as houses, badger sets, war bunkers and space ships ... ' (Lorraine 2003).

Conclusion

What do trainee teachers learn from playground observation?

> Teachers need to be aware of both their pupils' passions and preoccupations and how these can be productive in enabling new meanings to be creative.   (Millard 2003: 7)

The DMU programme has run for four years. The third year ITT trainees define literacy for themselves through their observation and recording of the games their pupils play and are able to move on to more grounded approaches to multiliteracy strategies in their fourth year. In undertaking this research they have:

- direct firsthand experience of children's creative thinking in action;
- a taste of small-scale ethnographic research;
- awareness of oral and multiple literacies from outside the classroom and of the vitality and control that children have when they absorb these into their own narrative creations;
- also awareness of children's sensitivity to modalities (ways of making meaning) other than the written text;
- broader definitions of speaking and listening and drama in curriculum English;
- the chance to make their own creative discoveries, to shape it and share it. 'It' being the wealth of children's literacy outside the classroom;
- the humility of the researcher when the children become the experts explaining the elements of their playground narratives and drama; and
- new insights on applying children's expertise outside the classroom to their literacy practices within the school.

Acknowledgements

Thanks to all Year 3 Language and Learning trainees 2000–2003 who have been involved in the close observation of so many children. Also to Louise Dolby (2001), Clare Cooper and Natasha Cunningham (2002), Lorraine Arends and Noreen Brophy (2003) for their contribution to this chapter.

References

Armstrong, M. (1997) 'The Leap of Imagination: an essay in interpretation', *FORUM*, 39 (2).

Bell, D. (2002) 'There's room for the arts', 'Opinion' in *Times Educational Supplement*, 18 October.

Browne, N. (1999) *Young Children's Literacy and the Role of Televisual Texts*. London: Falmer Press.

DfEE (2000) *Curriculum Guidance for the Foundation Stage*. London: QCA.

Erikson, E. (1965) cited in Kitson, N. '"Please Miss Alexander: will you be the robber?" Fantasy play: a case for adult intervention' in Moyles, J. (ed.) *The Excellence of Play*. Buckingham: Open University Press.

Kress, G. (2003) *Literacy in the New Media Age*. London: Routledge.

Marsh, J. (2003) 'Contemporary models of communicative practice: Shaky foundations in the foundation stage?', *English in Education*, 37 (1).

Marsh, J. and Millard E. (2000) *Literacy and Popular Culture. Using Children's Culture in the Classroom*. London: Paul Chapman.

Millard, E. (2003) 'Towards a literacy of fusion: new times, new teaching and learning?', *Reading*, April.

Moyles, J. (ed.) (1994) *The Excellence of Play*. Buckingham: Open University Press.

Opie, I. (1994) *The People in the Playground*. Oxford: Oxford University Press.

Paley, V. (1984) *Boys and Girls: Superheroes in the Doll Corner*. London: The University of Chicago Press Ltd.

Steedman, C. (1985) *The Tidy House: little girls' writing*. London: Virago.

Tyrell, J. (2001) *The Power of Fantasy in Early Learning*. London: Routledge/Falmer.

Whitehead, M. (1997) *Language and Literacy in the Early Years*, 2nd edn. London: Paul Chapman.

Chapter 4

Literacy, creativity and popular culture

Margaret Perkins

Over recent years there has been much training and writing on the subject of literacy teaching. The National Literacy Strategy *Framework for Teaching* (DfEE 1998) shows how literacy learning 'should' develop through the primary years and teachers have been inundated with support on 'how to' teach the National Literacy Strategy (NLS). Careers have been created around the implementation of the strategy and its impact has been seen in improving test results. Yet, there is still a group of children for whom literacy in school remains beyond their grasp. Luke (1998) argues that for too long the debates around literacy have been centred on method. He says that this debate

> presupposes that the literacy-related problems encountered by students and teachers in classrooms are indeed questions of method, questions that can be resolved by finding the right method.

There were many children like Ben, aged seven, who rushed to collect the latest Harry Potter book from the postman at 7 o'clock on a Saturday morning and spent an hour engrossed in it, reading text which might have been thought to be 'too difficult' for him. His school reading book remained in his folder where it had languished for several days. Comber (1998) describes Alan, saying, 'school literacy activities appear to cause Alan extreme physical discomfort and to put it bluntly he typically avoided what he could'. Ben and Alan are not alone: children for whom 'our existing theories of literacy will not do' (Bearne and Kress 2001).

We need maybe to move away from our fixation with method to consider the nature of the literacy we are teaching. Dombey (2002) describes an essential element of literacy learning as imaginative engagement 'with other ways of seeing the world' and this seems to be one way in which we need to bring creativity into our literacy teaching. Millard (2003) states that children are increasingly multimodally literate whilst their teachers remain constrained by the limits of print. She goes on to argue that we need, what she describes as a 'transformative pedagogy...fusing aspects of school requirements and children's interests into what becomes both a more tasty and a more nourishing diet' (p. 6).

The use of popular culture may be one way in which we can catch the interest of children like Ben and Alan and so enable them to engage with literacy practices in a more meaningful way. The work of writers such as Marsh and Millard (2000), Dyson (1997) and Bromley (2002) is now well known and in classrooms we can find evidence of much of their work. Lambirth (2003) however found that many teachers held a real aversion to the use of popular culture in the classroom. He proposes that this might be due to the power of the current model of literacy focusing on skills acquisition, resulting in the teachers not seeing the potential of popular culture for literacy learning. Many of the teachers in Lambirth's sample also expressed a real distaste for the content.

O'Brien (1997) echoes this view when she claims that the use of popular culture in the classroom is nearly always paired with the use of the term 'critical literacy' with the implication that it is fine to include popular culture in the curriculum as long as it is critiqued. Indeed, the work of Marsh and Millard (2000) suggest using popular culture as a way of confronting stereotypes and exploring issues such as good versus evil. There is more to it than this alone suggests. It is not just the content of the literacy practices that need to be transformed but the literacy itself.

Luke (Luke and Carrington 2002) defines three different types of literacy. Parochial literacy is that which is local and literacy practices serve to reproduce the status quo. Fantasy literacy takes the reader and writer out of the local, introduces other discourse and suspends their current position. Globalised literacy involves engagement with other worlds and takes the reader into analysis of all texts in relation to each other. It is my argument here that the use of popular culture needs engagement in fantasy literacy. Young children are taken out of the parochial school world of text types and are placed within a world in which symbolic representation holds other meanings. How does this work in practice?

Trading cards

A trainee teacher in her final school experience was working with a Year 1 group of children in a large suburban infant school. The year group was set by ability and she was working with the lowest ability group. She felt that part of the reason for the children's low level of achievement in literacy was the fact that the content of the daily literacy lesson was not immediately relevant to them. She wanted to engage the children with what was happening, to make it more exciting and appropriate to their interests. These were children who were already deemed to be falling behind within the school system.

She began the lesson by bringing out a large box containing a variety of trading cards; every possible type was in the box ranging from Yugio to Pokémon, Harry Potter to flower fairies. The children were excited because normally these were 'not allowed' in school. Immediately there was much discussion and sharing of information. The children became the experts, telling the adults what each element of the card meant. They knew what was signified by each symbol on the card and 'translated' it into a language or mode that the adults could understand. It was the teacher's aim that the children should explore the purposes of print and this they certainly did, explaining what each word signified. That was an important characteristic of what they did; they were not decoding the print in the sense of making a sound-symbol correspondence but were identifying what each element signified.

The teacher then focused on the names of the characters – looking at the pictures, identifying key features and seeing what the names told you about the character. This shared reading lesson took the form of a sophisticated analysis with both inferential and evaluative reading. How do you know if a character is a goodie or a baddie? What clues are there? The children showed themselves to be experienced readers of this type of text.

The lesson then moved on to shared writing. Under the direction of the class, the teacher drew a character on the whiteboard – the children discussed, described, and negotiated. They then talked with talk partners – thinking of a name for the character and justifying their choice in relation to the picture and the predicted behaviours of the character according to the picture.

In the independent time each child was asked to design his or her own card and think of and write a name. The children worked hard, all engaged in what they were doing. When it came to the writing they thought hard about the spelling and there was a lot of discussion around phonemic awareness. There was also much talk about how literacy works – what the name tells the reader.

During the plenary the children were again in role of expert. They described the sort of games that could be played with these cards; told how each card has its own value and how a player knows which is a good one to have. Some children even included elements of this on the design of their own card. They were given a challenge for the next time – think about a game you could play with your cards. Can you put your card with a friend's card to make a better game? As they left the classroom, the children were already sharing ideas and creating narratives around their cards.

Millard (2003) argues that 'critical literacy will remain only a theoretical ideal unless connected to a pedagogical practice that ensures that it becomes embedded in children's preferred modes of responding to, and producing, all manner of texts'. And that children need, 'access to a variety of ways of telling, designing and making and the opportunity to engage in meaningful dialogue in relation to their preferred modes and dispositions'. I want to consider this lesson in the light of these comments.

The passions and preoccupations of the children dominated the lesson and this resulted in a very real engagement on their part with the literacy practices. They had prime access to the meanings and for the most part the adults relied on the children's interpretation and explanation to gain full access; the children were the gatekeepers.

Secondly, in this activity the children were working within what was for them an authentic context. The acquisition and practice of literacy skills was certainly present and yet subsumed within a purpose which had a priority and importance in the eyes of the children.

Thirdly, the children were given the authority to shape and transform meanings. 'A transformative pedagogy would allow the children to explore aspects of their own identities and to be provided with spaces where they can choose whom to persuade or entertain on their own terms' (Millard 2003). In this literacy event the children were certainly working on their own terms; they were taking something which was an important part of their lives outside and exploring how it worked. In so doing they were coming to an understanding of the relationship between different symbolic systems and using them for themselves – surely an essential element in the process of becoming literate.

It could be argued that activities such as this are just changing the content of the activity to something which the children enjoy and that there is no difference in the literacy practised. However, it is more than this. The children were aware, implicitly if not otherwise, of the particular functions literacy served within the mode of trading cards. In allowing them to take control the teacher was using the structure of the daily literacy lesson to explore different types of literacy. Thus, children who were used to struggling and achieving limited success were placed in a position of authority. Traditional roles in relation to knowledge and understanding were subsumed. The teacher needed to understand this fully but in acknowledging the expertise of the children she transformed and so strengthened the learning potential of the activity.

The children became accountable for their own decisions. No longer was their achievement in literacy judged as successful or otherwise by criteria which were externally imposed and originated from a literacy practice embedded in the culture of schooling. The children were making choices about the names of their designed characters and how the name represented the pictorial representation or revealed hidden aspects of the character. The teacher was helping the children to make such decisions and selections but the children were responsible for their characters and their actions and were able to justify them.

Lambirth (2003) sees the pleasure which children gain from using popular culture as the basis of the fear which many teachers have about using these texts within the classroom. Bakhtin's (1968) idea of carnival can be seen in the turning upside down of expected norms and values. In introducing such texts into the classroom a teacher is validating a literacy where adult norms are transgressed. Some of the children delighted in giving their invented creatures names which would not normally be acceptable in the safe controlled world of the classroom. The 'frisson' of pleasure this gave children (Barthes 1975) added to the power of the learning potential.

Spiderman poems

The same trainee teacher, on another occasion, talked with her children about Spiderman. Their comments and knowledge about Spiderman drew on a range of sources from the latest film (which incidentally has a category 12 rating but was known in great detail by these 5- and 6-year-olds) to comics, toys, advertisements and videos. The words they knew and the images they invoked were powerful. The children wrote their poems, mainly using emergent writing, with no fear of transcriptional errors. The poems were read to the class and as the children read, the adults in the room made notes for later reference. Here are some of the poems:

> Spiderman is webby
> Spiderman is brave and strong
> Spiderman fights the goblin
> And the building is on fire.

James is referring to powerful images he knows from the film. Look at the word 'webby' he has created to describe not just what Spiderman does but what he sees as an essential characteristic of Spiderman. Edward again identifies the essence of Spiderman:

> Spiderman is a superhero
> Spiderman is good versus villains

Kai in his poem, seems to have identified the dilemma Peter Parker finds himself in. He is Peter Parker the person and yet he is also a spider:

> Spiderman is webby
> Spiderman is Peter Parker
> Spiderman is a hero
> And he is a tarantula.

This was a lively lesson and afterwards Pam, the trainee teacher, wrote in her evaluation:

> They were leaping about being Spiderman whenever I turned my back. They had a writing frame 'Spiderman is . . . ' and were asked to fill in the last word of as many lines of their poem as they wanted to. When I asked the teaching assistants what they thought, I had two comments. 'Had I learned the hard way why teachers don't do anything too "popular"'? Oh dear, I'm afraid I haven't. And 'Did you see C.P.?' No – he wasn't climbing up the wall – he was writing.

There are two issues here. First, the teaching assistants were echoing many of the views which Lambirth heard in his conversations with teachers. The children were 'being' Spiderman – they were revelling in the freedom and pleasure or 'jouissance' of taking something they knew which they saw as being something slightly subversive and using it in the classroom. The adults saw this as 'losing control' and were unwilling to allow this to happen.

Secondly, C.P. was a child who was usually very unwilling to do anything in a literacy lesson and consequently needed one-to-one attention. In this lesson however, he was writing:

> Spiderman is webby
> Spiderman is strong
> Spiderman is funny
> And he is never wrong!

This is a very successful piece of writing with a strong sense of rhythm, rhyme and theme from a child who usually underachieved.

Pam went on to write in her reflection on this lesson:

> If becoming 'literate' is not just about acquiring a body of knowledge (i.e. knowing a lot of literature) which it surely isn't, if it's not just about text level objectives; if being literate is something to do with having the power (potential) of a language at your command and the language is the language of a culture ... then figures of popular culture, e.g. Spiderman and the rest which naturally find a place in the language, surely have a part to play in our children's literacy.

> That vision of red and black, leaping from building to building, all that agility and those physical/visual thrills – should be able to find a place in their language development. Why should we let all that enthusiasm be reduced to mock fighting in the playground – why not let it inform their writing. I can think of a whole host of words for a 'word web' on Spiderman. Spiderman is ... lithe, agile, powerful, brave, fast and fearless, self-righteous and insanely egotistical.

Conclusion

What can we take from these isolated examples which we can apply to our teaching?

- Kress (2003) argues that in the new way of thinking about literacy, new definitions of meaning are required which include the idea of creativity. Meaning-making must involve the possibility of transforming (reshaping the form of) the resources 'in relation to the needs of the interests of the 'sign-maker' (p. 36). In the classroom this means that we need to understand different ways of expressing meaning and incorporate these into the literacy of schooling. Alphabetic writing is no longer the dominant means and we must consider the impact of 'image' on meaning-making.

- Pleasure, in its widest sense, is a core aspect of popular culture; its subversity allows the norms and expectations of traditional pathways to be turned upside down and inside out in a carnavalesque exploration of what can be done. The boundaries are being extended and broken in all modes of communication in society and we need to reflect this in school. It is no longer enough to reflect only the uses and means of communication of 20 years ago. The challenges today are greater and require more creativity on the part of the meaning-maker.

- The role of the teacher as the expert is now not always valid. Teachers must become co-learners and feel confident to share the role of expert with the children. More important than ever is the need to know and recognise the knowledge and skills the children possess and the ways in which they make meaning outside the home. I began this chapter by describing Ben working hard to read the latest Harry Potter. Ben is seven and loves superheroes, particularly Superman. He subscribes to a Superman comic; he has many videos of Superman ranging from the original 1920s' cartoons to the latest films; he watches all representations of Superman on the television from 'The New Adventures of Superman' to 'Smallville'. He is able to discuss in great detail the different portrayal of Superman in each of these and to do a sophisticated textual and historical analysis. He is able to 'read' the moving images and discuss what and how meaning is conveyed. He is not alone among his peers. Many conversations along these lines are held amongst them and these are then translated into their play, in which 'texts' of amazing creativity are created and occasionally recorded.

The challenge to us as teachers is to harness this creativity and take it into the classroom, transforming not only the content of our literacy lessons but our notions of literacy and our ideas of pedagogy.

Acknowledgements

My thanks to Pam Gardiner for her willingness to share her work with me and to the children for their work.

References

Bakhtin, M. (1968) *Rabelais and his world* (translated by H. Iswolsky). Cambridge: MIT Press.
Barthes, R. (1975) *The Pleasure of the Text* (translated by R. Miller). New York: Hill and Wang.
Bearne, E. and Kress, G. (2001) 'Editorial', *Reading* 35 (3).
Bromley, H. (2002) 'Meet the Simpsons', *The Primary English Magazine*, 7 (4).
Comber, C. (1998) *'Coming, Ready or Not! Changing what Counts as Early Literacy'*. Keynote address to the Seventh Australia and New Zealand conference on the first years of school, The Australian National University, Canberra.
DfEE (1998) National Literacy Strategy *Framework for Teaching*. London: DfEE.
Dombey, H. (2002) 'Patterns of interaction between teachers, children and texts in successful literacy learning'. Paper presented at 19th World Congress on Reading, Edinburgh.

Dyson, A. H. (1997) *Writing Superheroes: contemporary childhood, popular culture and classroom literacy*. New York: Teacher's College Press.

Kress, G. (2003) *Literacy in the New Media Age*. London: Routledge.

Lambirth, A. 'They get enough of that at home: understanding aversion to popular culture in schools', *Reading*, 37 (1), 9–13.

Luke, A. (1998) 'Getting over method: literacy teaching as work in "new times"', *Language Arts*, 75 (4), 305–13.

Luke, A. and Carrington, V. (2002) 'Globalisation, Literacy, Curriculum Practice' in Fisher, R., Lewis, M. and Brooks, G. (eds) *Language and Literacy in Action*. London: Routledge/Falmer.

Marsh, J. and Millard, E. (2000) *Literacy and Popular Culture: using children's culture in the classroom*. London: Paul Chapman.

Millard, E. (2003) 'Towards a literacy of fusion: new times, new teaching and learning?', *Reading*, 37 (1), 3–8.

O'Brien, J. (1997) 'The critical and the popular in current English curriculum documents'. Paper presented at the Australian Association for Research in Education Annual National Conference, Brisbane.

Chapter 5
DARE to Quack

Rebecca Sinker and
Victoria de Rijke

'Play is not in the activity or the appearance of play but in the person performing the activity and whether they are experiencing playfulness.'   (Mihaly Czikszentmihalyi)

FIGURE 5.1 Playing with vowel sounds and face shapes

This chapter looks at two CD-ROMs developed at Middlesex University in collaboration with arts and school partners both of which have play at their centre and draw on interdisciplinary models for their creative inspiration. The Digital Art Resource for Education (DARE) is an art and education resource which explores a host of ideas around play and performance, space and place, and language and translation, for children aged from 5 to 10 years old. Co-produced by Middlesex and the Institute of International Visual Arts, it features video, voices, drawings and other artworks by children from Columbia School and a range of international artists. The Quack-project asks the question 'Do ducks quack in the same way all over the world?' It features the voices of nursery children from over 20 London primary schools, making animal noises in a range of languages which reflect London's diversity. It also features electroacoustic music by modern composers Karlheinz Stockhausen and John Levack Drever.

Though these CDs have differences in terms of content, they were both designed for use with young children and are the outcomes of creative partnerships (established long before the term was hijacked for an Arts Council funding scheme!) between artists, arts institutions, educational institutions and pupils learning from each other, developing work through a collective process of action research, drawing on the best of everyone's imagination. Both these CDs contain material not normally made accessible (e.g. the work of contemporary artists and composers) as a deliberate strategy to raise expectation and expand the often somewhat limited classroom experience of these subject fields. The paucity of culturally diverse, avant garde ICT, art and music materials seem to us to have limited teachers' confidence to play as well as children's understanding of the spectrum of language possibilities.

Another pedagogic principle underpinning these projects is that they are process not product led – about the-way-of-making becoming what-gets-made. As Hollands has said, 'Art is what you make of it' (see note 1). For example, the design and content of the DARE resource were formed by the ideas and materials which emerged from school-based workshops with artists Maria Amidu and Barby Asante, where children were encouraged to think outside the traditional frameworks of the classroom and beyond the usual subject divisions. These collaborative weekly workshops introduced broad cultural themes such as play and performance, space and place, language and translation, where the artists worked with the children to develop ideas and produce artifacts which explored those themes, using old and new technologies. This way of working thus became the navigational principle for the programmers of the CD-ROMs, who continued to be informed by the children's responses to the developing content and structure, through participant design research principles. The open-ended nature of the CDs could appear to some as unfinished – in much the same way that many adults view children's work – but that is the point. It is for the user to provide alternative starting points and endings.

Within this particular project, the experience of working in dialogue with professional artists and designers both validated the children's opinions and provided an opportunity to explore forms and ideas which broadened their notion of art and language. It valued their creative input and brought their different experiences into play in a context that emphasised the importance of collective contribution. This extract is from a session where two Year 3 pupils were playing with and giving feedback to the *Translation* section of the developing CD-ROM.

Adult:	OK, try that... try the cat.
	(Computer miaow)
Adult:	What do you think this is about?
Girl :	A cat purring.
Adult:	A cat purring?
Boy:	Miaowing.
Adult:	... What do you think that writing's all about?
Girl:	About how to pronounce 'cat'.
Adult:	How you pronounce 'cat'. Where?
Girl:	All round the world – like, you've got Italy... Italian, like how you pronounce it in different languages.
Adult:	That's right. Now what would you like this page to do? Is it all right that it just explains it, or do you think it should have more on it?
Girl:	Like say 'cat'.
Adult:	You think it should say how to pronounce it?
Both:	Yeh...
Adult:	So... so if it said, for instance, 'This is how you say "cat" in Italian,' and then you click on 'Italian' and you could get it?
Boy:	Yeh. You hear how it says it, like...
Girl:	Yeh, 'cos some things you can't pronounce, you don't understand how you pronounce it.
Adult:	That's right, yes. Do you speak any other languages?
Both children speak together: I've learnt French. Bengali.	
Adult:	Do you know how to say 'cat' in Bengali?
Boy:	*Bilai*.
Adult:	*Bilai*. Shall we see if we've got it on there?... Bengali. Oh, it's different. It says *beral* or *manul* Is that... is that not right?
Boy:	Yeah, it's... er... is that the pron... er... is it like, er, when it miaows?
Adult:	No, it isn't the sound it makes, it's actually the word for 'cat'.
Boy:	Oh. No it's not.
Adult:	No, you don't say it like that, you say *bi*... What did you say?
Boy:	*Bilai*.
Adult:	Can we record you saying that?

Creative criticism of the work is another ongoing component, which can keep the material alive and fluid and acts against the more fixed interpretation of texts. Our best hopes are that some of the responses to DARE and Quack take non-verbal forms: pieces of music, drawings, performance, many away from the screen (and hopefully making a mess!). In this way, the CDs are intended to stimulate metaphoric non-literal, non-linear responses – in the way we can all react to art and music. Metaphor saves the human race from the awful possibility of things being only as they are signalled in surface language. As Hartley says in *The Go-Between*, 'To see or hear things as they really are – what an impoverishment!' (Hartley 1961: 251) or as Miles Davis put it, 'Don't play what's there, play what's not there' (see note 2).

In 1979, Dr Kirschenblatt-Gimblett pointed out that 'we have underestimated the nature of ordinary language and made too strong a dichotomy between instrumental and referential language on the one hand, and play language on the other.' She talked of wanting to:

> set up a continuum and to array various types of speech along it: at one end of the continuum you have the guy in the control tower in the airport giving instructions for how to land a plane. You really don't care how he speaks as long as he communicates clearly. At the other end of the continuum you have the idea it's not *what* you say but *how* you say it...a continuum is more useful than a dichotomy. (Kirshenblatt-Gimblett 1979: 237)

When did we lose sight (and sound) of this continuum? If all our language experience is reduced to the National Literacy Strategy and phonics reduced to a mechanism of oral accuracy, then will we produce a nation entirely made up of air traffic controllers? Surely we would want air traffic controllers to be precise at work and playful at home?

The principle of returning to a more holistic language continuum is behind both the DARE and Quack projects, partly because we both work across the disciplines of education, art and English. Is it the artificial separation of knowledge into curriculum subjects that is the problem or the rigidity of this approach? If you read the National Curriculum (NC) or any of its strategies as a set of instructions it becomes dogma for the teacher and drill for the pupils.

Teachers: why not just skim read all curriculum material and look for creative opportunities rather than rules?

The emphasis placed on phonics as the foundation for early reading and writing is fully evident in the National Literacy Strategy (NLS) and its attendant schemes such as 'Progression in Phonics' (Pips), 'Jolly Phonics' (or even perhaps 'No-Fun-At-All Phonics'). The NLS phonics online and CD resource to all teachers and trainees includes material which could be used playfully. 'Do Cats Bark?' reads one flashcard. Whilst interpreted in different ways by different teachers, when put into practice as a drill, whole class phonics teaching can veer away from creativity towards the pursuit of accuracy and uniformity. Yet we should not forget that the English language is inconsistent, even within itself! What informs both DARE and Quack is the further concern that in a multilingual society, children's language differences need to be called into play as a rich resource within the whole field of communication.

On the DARE CD the *Translation* section is where we discover the work of artists and children who are playing with making sounds, languages and meanings. Japanese artist Takahiko Iimura sounds out vowels – common to Japanese and English – while playfully amplifying cultural differences through his manipulated video visuals. 'Just as a vowel has no meaning by itself, so there is no need to translate it and I try to let the vowel speak a universal significance by itself. A letter or character may be national or regional but a sound is more universal. So even if one does not understand Japanese, one can immediately recognise a voice and relate it to an image' (Iimura 1998: 37). Children across Key Stages 1 and 2 and with diverse language backgrounds react immediately to the humour of this work and are impelled to play alongside. In other words, they are intrinsically motivated. It is important to recognise – as Iimura does – that speaking or sounding is a creative act in itself. This notion of similarity and difference in languages and the relationships between words, sounds, ideas and meanings is key to developing formal language skills – but to explore these ideas fully and creatively, children need to play with them, to break rules as well as learn them, to interpret and try out new meanings for language in all its social contexts.

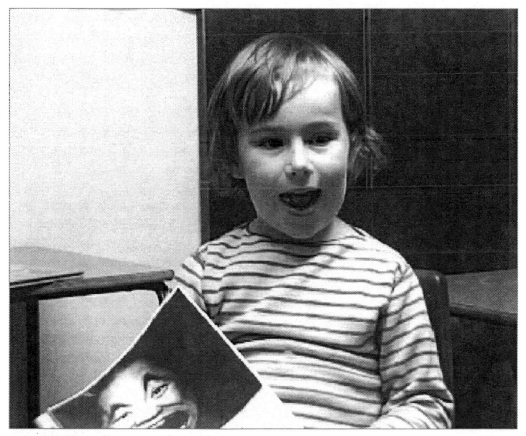

FIGURE 5.2 Watching Takahiko Iimura's *AIUEONN: Six Features* (1993)

During the developmental workshops with the artists, the children were continually invited to give their own responses to both concepts and verbal and visual materials. During one of these workshops with the Reception class, Maria Amidu was showing postcards of artists' work to small groups of children. She showed an image of the sculptural installation *Cold Dark Matter: an exploded view (1991)* by Cornelia Parker, which depicts the fragments of an exploded garden shed, suspended in space with a light bulb in the centre, casting a web of shadows on the walls (see note 3). Marzarna immediately exclaimed 'Incy Wincy Spider here!' and pointed to the centre of the exploded shards. Raswana (who, like her twin Marzarna, spoke very little English at this stage) then pointed to the image and said something in Bengali. We asked Hena, the interpreter, to ask her what she thought the image was and Raswana replied in Bengali, 'it's a broken house'. These children were able to draw on the various language forms available to them, visual, verbal and metaphoric, to express both imaginative and descriptive responses to an image of an unfamiliar contemporary art work.

Similarly, when taping nursery children making animal sounds in their mother tongue languages for the Quack-project, when asked to sound an English cockerel, Grace reproduced an uncanny imitation of the sound a cockerel makes rather than the onomatopoeic word, 'cocka-doodle-doo'. She then added 'ull-doo' to the end of the sound, thus conveying the total complexity of her understanding. Cockerels make a sound true to themselves as well as having sounds and meanings attributed to them by humans. This is also demonstrated by the comment of another child, Claude, after a dog barked at him: 'That dog called me Woof!'.

What both CDs exemplify (in their development and in their use) is the complexity of language understanding in very young children: almost certainly well beyond our expectations. Developing Chomsky's theories that language facility is innate to all humans, the MIT cognitive scientist Stephen Pinker argues that 'the crux of the argument is that complex language is universal because *children actually reinvent it*, generation after generation – not because they are taught, not because they are generally smart, not because it is useful to them, but because they can't help it' (Pinker 1994: 32). This would suggest that creative invention is innate rather than taught. A creative curriculum is a tautology; it is how we interpret it that is creative. The way that Bengali-speaking children used literal description in mother-tongue and nursery-rhyme in English as an additional language, suggests that linguistic playfulness is conceptual and can operate when still at the early stages of mastering a new language. Young children's engagement with animal sounds supports this too: when a group was asked what it meant that an English duck says 'Quack' but a Dutch frog also says 'Kwaak', they replied: 'Well, they both live in ponds where it's cold and rainy and they could talk together and be friends'.

Composer Karheinz Stockhausen, featured on the Quack CD, describes how he came to create *Hymnen*, partly inspired by a growing understanding of national disharmony. He describes listening to programmes from all over the world on his radio and recording over 150 national anthems. He began to experiment with them and the extract included on the Quack-project is one such experiment: with sounds of children playing, ducks and the French national anthem (bear in mind the French national symbol is a cockerel, so using ducks is deliberate irony):

> I took the sound of: 'little boys shouting "Hi, come here!" – speeded up, and I moved this sound up again in speed until it sounds like ducks. I used an actual recording of swamp ducks, and you don't notice when the real ducks are continuing from the human voices. I then took one small duck – just a Quack Quack – and put her on the machine, and she quacks the beginning of the *Marseillaise*: Quack-quak-quak-qua-qua, qua-qua, cah cah cah qua quaaa... I'm interested in revealing how, at a special moment, a human sound is that of a duck and a duck's sound is the silver sound of shaking metal fragments. Many of the fairy tales are about this: the straw that the miller's daughter has to weave into gold in *Rumpelstiltskin* for example... And that's the theme of *Hymnen* (see note 4).

When Stockhausen needs to describe the transformational power of music 'in revealing how, at a special moment, a human sound is that of a duck and a duck's sound is the silver sound of shaking metal fragments', he turns to metaphor. There is no such thing as a standard quack. On the Quack CD, children can compose making choices of language, animal and position, creating changes in pitch and melody. Composition is therefore visual as well as aural and both can work metaphorically or stand for something else. Metaphor is what goes beyond language at the literal, dictionary level, in our speech and song and imaginative writing. As the French writer Roland Barthes said: 'The grain is in the body in the voice as it sings, the hand as it writes...' (Barthes 1977: 188). In a sense it is this 'grain' or texture of sound which makes the Iimura and Stockhausen work so rich and engaging for adults and children. We accept that many people may not have heard of Iimura or Stockhausen but this is precisely why we have chosen these artists, acknowledging the limits of what is accessible in the form of teaching resources.

Teachers: why not draw on your own particular passions in arts and music, as well as those of the children in your classroom, instead of commercially produced curriculum materials?

The interface for *Translation* on the DARE CD, represents a dynamic space of communication where signs float, intersect and audibly react to the user. As one child described it, 'It's like all these little people coming out, all these objects coming to life.' It represents the continuum of speech play to verbal art plus it extends that to a wider spectrum including visual and kinaesthetic forms. Following a gaming model, the user has to literally capture or grasp the elements, which also alludes to the way one picks up a foreign language. There are random, rule-governed and voluntary elements all juxtaposed on a single, interactive page: languages in plural. The whole CD-ROM employs a discovery-based model rather than instructional model of learning – *what happens if I try this?* rather than *do this then this* – responding to the way that young children often approach multimedia texts, when left to their own devices.

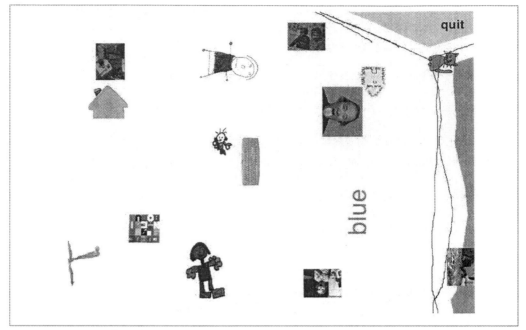

FIGURE 5.3 Interface for the *Translation* section of the DARE CD-ROM

FIGURE 5.4 Interface for the Quack field

The field in the Quack-project has many levels to it. It is green, like grassland, or a literal field for farming and pasture. It is a field of classification: it has representation of different fields or provinces of language, all of which are spoken in London, speaking for different animals in London, often in city farms. Like a city farm or the city itself, the Quack-project is a multilingual environment, and as such can be both playful as well as a battlefield, a field of action, where languages differ and jostle for supremacy (who quacks the loudest, as Darwin would have it) (see note 5). The Quack-project field is a language field or a field of literacy made up of phonic, syntactic and semantic elements (of phonemes, or sound-parts, of grammars and of meanings). Though it is a single space or enclosure for those languages, this field is a multilingual territory, full of diversity and complexity and, no doubt, mistakes! It is a research field (a field of inquiry) for field study; a discursive field. Most importantly, it is a metaphoric field, which stands for all these things and hopefully many more.

Both the interfaces described, encourage play, promote an awareness of shifting sound and image values and use electronic languages which speak metaphorically about what multiliteracies might best mean in a digital age. Digital technologies hold this potential for multiple literacies, but still tend to speak one language, one ideology. (Are we all using Microsoft products, for example?)

Returning to Kirshenblatt-Gimblett's notion of 'the continuum', this time in relation to the place and use of ICT in learning, we believe it is vital to open out the use of ICT beyond a self-contained subject or activity. In other words, not viewing ICT as an isolated task or set of skills to develop, nor thinking of it as a separate mediated space for thinking and doing, but rather as a node in an interconnected network of learning which extends beyond the screen and the classroom.

Teachers: why not use your digital resources as the trigger for creative writing or speaking as well as the focus of critical and analytical thinking, e.g. why do you think the author (producer) wrote/designed this in this way?

Huizinga believed that play is at the heart of all culture and a prerequisite for creative work in art and literature (Huizinga 1949). If play and creativity are implicated in one another, then the recent concern for creative and critical thinking being essential parts of the National Curriculum for England must logically include play. 'Creative thinking skills: these enable pupils to generate and extend ideas, to suggest hypotheses, to apply imagination and to look for innovative outcomes.' (DfES 2002).

While useful, this description omits the social context of critical thinking and particularly the dialogic element, where we examine our own beliefs and consider other people's perspectives. One of the aims of both the DARE and Quack CD-ROMs is to foster the ability to de-centre – to see things from another point of view – and the use of work by other children, in the context of ICT resources, is particularly effective for this. If learning is a social process, as Vygotsky suggests, surely it needs to reflect the society we are part of, in all its diversity and complexity? Does it not also follow, as

Kirshenblatt-Gimblett argues, that languages and literacies exist on a continuum which includes the precise, the poetic and the playful?

It is not by accident that both the DARE and Quack projects chose to draw upon language elements within early years environments. It is in the Nursery and Reception classrooms that the relative freedom remains for multimodal interdisciplinary, exploratory and playful ways of working. Perhaps upper Key Stage 1 and Key Stage 2 teachers need to free up their practices and revisit the importance of language and social development through play. Go on, 'quack' – we dare you . . . (see note 6).

Notes

1 Howard Hollands, Principal Lecturer Art and Design Education, Middlesex University, as quoted on the DARE website (www.dareonline.org).
2 This widely used quote is attributed to Miles Davis, the jazz musician.
3 This work can be viewed on the Tate website: (http://www.tate.org.uk/colddarkmatter/default.htm).
4 Karlheinz Stockhausen online interview (BBC Radio 4, 2001).
5 I am referring here to Charles Darwin's notion of the survival of the fittest, though his model for the way evolution is determined has been challenged many times since.
6 For further information, or to order a copy of either CD, contact ADULT Sinker (DARE) on dare@mdx.ac.uk or Victoria de Rijke (Quack) on www.kahve-house.com/society/shop, telephone 020 8362 6369.

References

Barthes, R. (1977) *Image, Music, Text*, p. 188. London: Fontana Press.
Cziksentmihaly, M. (1979) in Dibb, M. (director/producers) *Play*. BBC Productions.
DfES (2002) http://www.nc.uk.net/learn_think.html (accessed 20.6.2003).
Hartley, L. P. (1961) *The Go-Between*. London: Penguin.
Huizinga, Johan (1949, 1980 printing) *Homo Ludens: a study of the play-element in culture*. London: Routledge and Kegan Paul.
Iimura, T. (1998) 'Identity in the video of Takahiko Iimura' in Keen, M. (ed.) *Frequencies: Investigations into Culture, History and Technology*, p. 37. London: Institute of International Visual Art.
Kirshenblatt-Gimblett, B. (1979) 'Speech play and verbal art' in Sutton-Smith, B. (ed.) *Play and Learning*, p. 237. New York: Gardner Press.
Pinker, S. (1994) *The Language Instinct*, p. 32. London: Penguin.

Video text

Iimura, T. (1993) *AIVEONN: Six features*.

Chapter 6

Creativity and picture books

Judith Graham

(*First published in the UKRA journal,* Reading, *July 2000. Reproduced by permission of Blackwell Publishers.*)

The relationship between words and pictures

Picture books are very special artefacts for children and occasionally they are perfect. My argument in this chapter is that picture books reach perfection when their creators are at their most disciplined. By this, I mean that the creators of perfect picture books have recognised that the two media in which they work (words and pictures) need not, and often should not, 'say' the same thing. The discipline comes in being able to let each medium do what it does best and cutting away duplication. What pictures do best is show – they show what characters look like, what they are doing and the setting in which they move. To some extent, they show us what characters are feeling. What words do best is name, locate in time, generalise and tell us what characters are saying or thinking. They can also tell us what happened earlier or what may happen later. Here is Maurice Sendak's explanation of the process: 'You must never illustrate exactly what is written. You must find a space in the text so that pictures can do the work. Then you must let the words take over where words do it best. It's a funny kind of juggling act' (Lanes 1980: 110).

The relationship exemplified

An example from the opening pages of *Where The Wild Things Are* will help us here. Sendak gives us a picture of a cat-suited young person who appears determined, grim or disgruntled. He is using an enormous claw hammer to knock an equally enormous nail into the wall. (The plaster is visibly cracking.) We see that he is standing on two fine books to gain the necessary height for his task. From the nail is hung a line to

FIGURE 6.1
Where The Wild Things Are ©
Maurice Sendak
(1963)

support some sort of tent. A toy dog hangs forlornly from the line. The words 'The night Max wore his wolf suit and made mischief...' give us the time, the child's name and gender, specific naming of the garment he is wearing and the generalisation that what he is doing is to be named as 'mischief'. The mischief is further exemplified when we turn the page and see Max terrorising his (real-life) dog.

FIGURE 6.2
Where The Wild Things Are ©
Maurice Sendak
(1963)

The third opening gives a very clear indication of the relative roles of words and pictures. We cannot know, however long or carefully we look at the picture, that Max's mother called him 'WILD THING!' nor that Max retorted, 'I'LL EAT YOU UP!' and it is also from the words only that his mother must have noted his angry retort and punished Max by withholding food. The absence of the mother in the illustration helps to confirm that the verbal exchange and the sending to bed have happened before the scene we are shown. Only words can summarise off-stage action. But the picture can give us the character's reactions to reported happenings. We see a still-defiant Max. We can also see he has been relocated to his bedroom and can sense that the closed door has just been firmly shut.

FIGURE 6.3
Where The Wild Things Are ©
Maurice Sendak
(1963)

How successful picture books promote readers' creativity

I shall also explore in this chapter the argument that, when picture book creators work in this most disciplined way, the resulting classic leaves a reverberating space in which the creativity of readers can find expression. If a picture book both shows and tells us everything, it leaves very little work for the reader to do and, though the story may be pleasing, it seldom goes on living in our minds. This is the challenge facing new writers as Perry Nodelman explains: 'The main difficulty facing new writers of texts for picture books is the understanding that they must leave visual information in the hands of their illustrators' (Nodelman 1988: 202). Where a book does make us search to bring word and image into a three-dimensional whole, we usually feel a rush of satisfaction that is often the outward sign of creativity. This creativity is not far from the dynamic response of which Wolfgang Iser speaks: 'As the reader uses various perspectives offered him by the text in order to relate the patterns...to one another, he sets the work in motion, and this very process results ultimately in the awakening of responses in himself' (Iser 1974: 275). I have always thought that David McKee's book *Not Now, Bernard!* has enjoyed its enormous popularity over 20 years, not simply because it is about a naughty boy and a monster, but because of its delicious ambiguity and the readerly satisfaction experienced as readers pull its spare text and its clever pictures into a whole. McKee has pitched the book superbly. Had he been a little more explicit, readers would have had little to be active and creative about; a little less explicit, and, for his intended audience, the overstrain would, again in Iser's (1974) words, mean that the reader would 'leave the field of play'.

From a teacher's point of view, the existence of books like this is of incalculable value. It is alarming that the National Literacy Strategy makes no direct reference to the place of picture books in children's development as readers. It is up to teachers to build on the evidence before their eyes: children return to picture books and in the process of their close inspections, they discover depths. They want to share discoveries and responses. Picture books are also, it seems to me, the books from which teachers discover their own most imaginative ideas flow. From these books they can devise their most creative activities. Margaret Meek has a term for it – 'imaginative looking'. 'Picture books' she says, 'are not simply privileged reading for or with children. They make reading for all a distinctive kind of imaginative looking' (Meek 1991: 116). I hope to show, through an exploration of books at present found in primary classrooms, that teachers and children can be caught up imaginatively through the creative talent of authors and illustrators.

Ginger

Ginger, written and illustrated by Charlotte Voake, won the Gold Medal for the Under 5 Category of the 1997 Smarties Prize and was shortlisted for the 1997 Emil/Kurt Maschler Award. In the story, we are introduced to Ginger, a 'lucky' cat with a pampered existence. One day, a small, playful kitten arrives. The kitten's antics, especially its occupation of his basket, drive Ginger from the house. The little girl eventually finds Ginger hiding under a bush in the garden and, regretting that the cats cannot be friends, she makes separate arrangements for each cat's eating and sleeping. However, both cats end up in the small cardboard box, intended for the kitten. Hostility is over, perhaps.

Written text and spare, uncluttered illustrations initially go along hand in hand. At one point however, we see the kitten destroying an arrangement of flowers, clawing the

The little girl
found him on the table
drinking some milk.

"You naughty kitten!" she said.

FIGURE 6.4 *Ginger* © Charlotte Voake (1997)

back of an elegant chair and drinking, not from a saucer, but from a jug of milk on the table. The written text is marvellously understated at these points and we can imagine Charlotte Voake paring her words down until she arrives at 'The kitten played with some flowers, then he found somewhere to sharpen his claws. The little girl found him on the table, drinking some milk.' As written, the kitten's behaviour is natural, at worst innocent. The pictures make us smile at the extra dimension of nuisance added.

Here is the reverberating space that teachers can exploit. Children will already have shown them the way by clamouring to tell tales of their cats' 'naughtiness'. Indeed several additional pages could be inserted into the story at this point and we could muse that Charlotte Voake could have used any one of the ideas. We can encourage children's creative responses by sharing the notion that writers and illustrators have had to make choices. Voake could have included, for instance, the kitten playing with wool or swinging on the curtains but she didn't. But if we want to stay close to the story as written, as an activity, we could add all the admonitions that might well have occurred at these points in the story. Thus, 'Oh kitten, why do you choose the very best chair on which to sharpen your claws? At least you might have chosen one which we haven't just re-covered.' This isn't an actual quote from a child but is very typical of the dialogue, or monologue, that children produce when role playing well-known stories. This kind of added dialogue lends itself to a shared writing activity where children's offerings can be scribed by the teacher after discussion of likely dialogue.

The image of the two cats squashed into one small cardboard box is left only to the illustration, as is the final image of the kitten playing with Ginger's tail and Ginger looking less sure that reconciliation was a good idea. Here again are two more gaps to fill. Role play followed again by shared writing would bring out the unwritten nuances of these pictures. One could, for instance, start off a little play, having first given names to the characters as they are nameless in Voake's text.

Sally: I don't believe it! Ginger, why are you in Dusty's cardboard box with her?
Ginger (purring loudly): Don't you know, Sally, all cats like cardboard boxes however small they are? And it's even better if you're squashed in with another cat, even Dusty.

Children could then be encouraged to add the next few lines.

Grandmother and I

Another picture book for the youngest readers is *Grandmother and I* by Helen E. Buckley, illustrated by Jan Ormerod. The written text existed as a poem before it was offered to Jan Ormerod who has added her emphasis and vision to the original words. Obviously, in a situation like this, the written text cannot be pared down or altered; it is up to the illustrator to find angles that will enrich the story and not merely reproduce the meaning of the words. In the written text, a child and grandmother are rocking back and forth in a rocking chair. The narrator (the girl) knows that whilst the laps of mothers, fathers and grandfathers have their uses, and whilst brothers and sisters provide backs if not laps, only grandmother's lap provides comfort on occasions when you are feeling poorly or being frightened by a storm or when the cat goes missing. A refrain ('We sit in the big chair/and rock back and forth, and back and forth. /And Grandmother hums little tunes. /And her shoes make a soft sound on the floor.') is repeated and the words 'back and forth' echo the movement of the rocking chair.

For Jan Ormerod, lover of cats (as can be deduced from her other picture books), the single line ('the cat's been gone for two days') about the missing cat may have been the spark which fired her imaginative interpretation of the poem. For the cat's story and the child's devotion to it are the heart of the illustrations. The cat is on the scene from the beginning, including cover and title page, until it is lost, and it is only through the illustrations that we know that the cat has returned.

The ground is covered in snow at the start of the story and the trees are bare but as the story progresses, blossom appears, snow-covered when the cat is missing, and in full flower on the cat's return. The season is not specified in the original poem. Here is the start of children's appreciation of symbolism in literature. Initially, symbolism is more readily grasped through illustration, as close readers of Anthony Browne's texts will tell you, as they, for instance, spot the facial mole that connects the step mother and the witch in *Hansel and Gretel*. Many child readers will be stimulated to express the most complex of thoughts as they inspect the pictures. They may start by noticing that Ormerod signifies winter conventionally by the clothes worn as well as by the snow, the bare trees, dark skies and the snowman built. They may end by speculating on the reasons why, by the end, winter is on its way to spring.

When a teacher comes to work on activities for this text, she will find that seeking the understatement in the text is likely to be a fruitful starting point. At one point, in the illustrations, the child narrator, whilst she is being piggy-backed by her brother, seems to notice a 'lost' poster for a dog pinned onto a tree. We can't read the words but we can guess what they say. Is the little girl looking at it? Her cat is not missing at this point in the story but perhaps she is thinking how terrible it would be if it were. Not long after that, her cat disappears. Children will often go straight to this part of the story, talking of when their animals have gone missing and what they did about it. It is a short step from this sharing of firsthand experiences, to the thought that perhaps this little girl also made a missing poster. A discussion of what needs to go into such a poster (cat description, contact number, reward) can feel like an authentic activity in the context of this story and lends itself to class, group and individual work.

Another area, where we can encourage children's creative responses, and one touched on in the earlier discussion of *Ginger*, is the notion that writers and illustrators have had to make choices. Buckley could have had our child narrator sitting on grandmother's lap for comfort for all sorts of other reasons but she chose feeling poorly, fear of a storm and grief over the missing cat. What other reasons might she have considered? Children will draw on their own fears for this (although they need not declare them as their personal worries). They may suggest retreating to the rocking chair and grandmother's lap when brothers and sisters won't let you join in their game, when you can't find your teddy bear or when you have been out-voted over a television programme. The youngest children will enjoy physically taking the rocking chair hot seat and announcing their reason for being there.

Six Dinner Sid

The final title to consider here is *Six Dinner Sid*, written and illustrated by Inga Moore. Sid, the cat, cunningly contrives to live with all six occupants of a terrace of houses in Aristotle Street. Thus he enjoys six dinners daily and although he has to accommodate the differing customs of all the householders, he basks in the attention that six people give him. Because Sid's owners do not speak to each other, they do not realise the deception. The day comes when Sid catches a cold and is taken to the vet – six times. Cough medicine is administered six times daily but the vet grows suspicious about six black cats all coming from Aristotle Street and alerts each of the owners. On appreciating the situation, Sid's owners are unforgiving and vow to restrict him to one meal a day. Sid is having none of this and goes off to live in Pythagoras Place where he is again adopted by six families, but as they talk to each other and know what is going on, they are quite happy to keep up Sid's regime.

When we turn to the illustrations, we see that Inga Moore has carefully built up the pictured detail about the different characters who live in Aristotle Street to provide rounded pictures of the characters about whom the written text is silent. Thus, for instance, we know that the occupant of Number 1 is female, has a garage though probably no car, gives Sid the name 'Scaramouche' and feeds him with fish. She is a keen gardener, is grey-haired and wears glasses, reads Kipling, is rather posh – she has velvet cushions with tassels – and an orange telephone. It should be possible to ask children to make a card game (where you collect sets) by collecting the pictured information for all six occupants and transferring it onto 'family' cards. This would entail careful looking on the part of the children and a move from what is pictured only to the expression of that information in words. For each of the six occupants, at least eight cards could be made and then collected as sets by players of the game.

The six-sided character of Sid is also exemplified in the pictures (as is his increasing belly size). Though the residents of Pythagoras Place are not so fleshed out, we can tell that there are families with children here, that they are a friendly lot and that the neighbourhood is mixed racially. Children can weave a narrative around the information presented.

FIGURE 6.5 *Six Dinner Sid*
© Inga Moore (1990)

It is a book that lends itself to so many creative responses. Unusually, there is no direct speech in this book but it is clear that lots of talking and thinking goes on. Look at the picture where the occupant of Number 4 is scratching Sid's ear. All the others are looking on jealously. We can imagine their thoughts or write them down in thought bubbles, remembering that each owner has his or her special name for Sid. The other times when talk must have been going on are when the vet has phone conversations with each owner and when the owners all get in a censuring circle round Sid. All these conversations can be imaginatively invented.

If Sid is clever enough to live in six homes and get fed six dinners, he must be clever enough to talk. So we can even imagine he has a friend in another street to whom he tells the story of a typical day in the houses of Aristotle Street. Only the pictures provide the content here. Sid, I'm sure, would be compelled to write an auto-biography one day and he'd also make a suitable candidate for a 'This is Your Life' TV programme, where he will doubtless have things to suggest about the relative merits of the folk in the two streets.

Some children on reading this book will immediately respond to the message that Inga Moore is delivering about the importance of neighbourly friendliness. Some may even sense a comment on social class. But to begin here would be to miss the fun of the book, and it is through exploring the book in other aspects, that all children have time to reach reflections on its deeper meanings.

Conclusion

In conclusion, I wish to counter what I imagine might be some criticisms of this way of working. Firstly, it may be regarded as too much like fun or rather too much like playing. But play is a compulsory element that all nursery schools must provide and the new National Curriculum is rather keen on in-role talk and writing and imagina-tive exploration of ideas and feelings. I would want to say that it is in structured simulations, empathy work, open-ended scenarios and improvisation that children discover a fluency and flair, a creativity, that eludes them all too often in much other work in the classroom. For persuasive accounts of the value of work of this type, I would refer readers to Lesley Hendry's chapter (in Styles, Bearne and Watson 1996) and to Jennie Carter's article (in *Reading*, July 1999). Secondly, I think as teachers we need to reclaim ground that has been shrouded in mist for too long. Creativity has had a poor press recently, suspected of obstructing the learning of skills. But involved, laterally thinking children do learn the 'basics' in this sort of work and many would argue that they learn the excitement and rewards of literacy more emphatically and lastingly through creative work rather than through more prosaic activities. Thirdly, if children are encouraged to work in these ways and in other problem-solving, open-ended and reflective ways, I cannot believe that they would not be all the better equipped for the uncertain future that the century is surely unfurling. Lastly, and to assert again my convictions about picture books, we can, through employment of picture books, bring a second and third teacher into the classroom. Authors and illustrators have done half our planning for us – and high-quality planning it is too – and we can piggyback on their talent and industry and use their books to jumpstart our own imaginations. Not to use these glorious and plentiful objects, designed absolutely for children but a delight to all, is truly to look a gift horse in the mouth.

References

Browne, A. (1981) *Hansel and Gretel*. London: Julia MacRae Books.

Buckley, H. and Ormerod, J. (1995) *Grandmother and I*. London: Viking.

Carter, J. (1999) The Power and the Story, *Reading*, 33 (2), 87–90.

DfEE (1998) *National Literacy Strategy Framework for Teaching*. London: Standards and Effectiveness Unit.

DfEE (1999) *English in the National Curricurum*. London: HMSO.

Hendry, L. (1996) *With the Wind Behind You* in Styles, M., Bearne, E. and Watson, V. *Voices Off*. London: Cassell.

Iser, W. (1974) *The Implied Reader*. Baltimore, Md.: Johns Hopkins University Press.

Lanes, S. (1980) *The Art of Maurice Sendak*. New York: Abradale Press.

McKee, D. (1980) *Not Now, Bernard!* London: Andersen Press.

Meek, M. (1991) *On Being Literate*. London: The Bodley Head.

Moore, I. (1990) *Six Dinner Sid*. London: Hodder and Stoughton.

Nodelman, P. (1988) *Words about Pictures: the narrative art of children's picture books*. Athens: University of Georgia Press.

Sendak, M. (1963) *Where The Wild Things Are*. London: The Bodley Head/Red Fox.

Styles, M., Bearne, E. and Watson, V. (1996) *Voices Off*. London: Cassell.

Voake, C. (1997) *Ginger*. London: Walker Books.

Two of the three books discussed in this article are from amongst the 30 which I consider in *Cracking Good Picture Books* (NATE 2004) which is intended for teachers working at Key Stages 1 and 2.

Chapter 7

Creative readers at Key Stage 2

Catriona Nicholson

In terms of literacy development, one of the primary tasks of a classroom teacher is to understand and extend children's responses to literary texts. The process begins in the early years of schooling and continues through the primary and secondary stages of education. However, in terms of teacher education and of the NLS guidelines the actual teaching of the *reading of literature* warrants a more prominent profile. In order to recognise and extend what Jonathan Culler (1975) called 'literary competence' in their pupils, not only should teachers be familiar with a wide range of literature for children (Aidan Chambers (1993) suggests a newly trained graduate should be familiar with 'a basic library' of 500 texts) but they should also have a basic understanding of the phenomenology of reading – of the diverse and complex ways in which readers bring meaning to texts.

Jon Stott (1994), referring to the value of literature for children, sees the teaching of the reading of literature as a developmental process:

> one in which each stage of the instruction can introduce reading skills that provide the foundations on which more complex ones are built. Specific stories can be chosen not only for their literary merit but also for introducing, developing or reinforcing response skills.

He identifies the dual function of well-chosen narrative texts:

> In reading stories, in understanding them and responding actively to them, children are not only developing their literary competencies, they are also fulfilling their need for narratives that better help them give shape and meaning to their own lives as individuals and members of their communities.

Stott's belief is echoed by the novelist Katherine Paterson (1989) who writes passionately about her task as a writer for children: 'I believe it is the job of a novelist to shape human experience so that a reader might be able to find not only order but meaning in a story.'

Children articulating response

Responding to a text is essentially an active, creative process and lies at the heart of literacy teaching. According to Harding (1977) 'response is a word that should remind the teacher that the experience of art is a thing of our making, an activity in which we are our own interpretive artist'. Encouraging children to 'articulate personal responses to literature, identifying why and how they are affected' (Year 6 term 1) is an objective required by the National Literacy Strategy (NLS) but one that is difficult to manage and achieve in large, mixed ability classes where the range of literary competency among pupils covers a wide spectrum of aptitude and developmental levels.

Faced with such a situation and hoping to generate and share reading responses with a class of 34 Year 6 children, I set about finding ways of ensuring that each child's contribution could be identified and, as Chambers (2001) describes, 'honourably reported'.

I had taught this particular class in their third year of primary school and therefore knew something of their individual reading histories and of the shared literature they had encountered. As readers we respond to literature in terms of our previous experience and our understanding of literary conventions. Although a few of these children still remained 'inexperienced' readers at the upper primary stage they were familiar with narrative structures and with a wide range of texts and authors. I was therefore optimistic about each child's ability to record, and later articulate, reader responses and set about planning for this whole class literacy project.

I wanted each child to read and to share responses to a novel. Because of the initial impact it had on me, and because I believed these children would respond to its themes and issues, I chose Katherine Paterson's 1977 Newbery Medal prizewinner *Bridge to Terabithia*. Set in Virginia and based closely on a real life experience in the author's family, it tells the story of a friendship between a young boy and girl, Jesse Aarons and Leslie Burke. Alongside daily commonplace encounters in school, they create through imaginative play, a world of their own in the local woods, calling it the kingdom of Terabithia and for a season they become its rulers. Unexpected tragedy ends the friendship and Jesse is left alone and, for a while, comfortless. Paterson's gift as a writer enables readers of all ages to empathise with Jesse's plight and to realise that his slow and painful recovery is built upon the rich legacy of Leslie's belief in him.

In the initial stages of introducing the idea of a shared class novel I needed to ensure that all the children had equal experience of this text. It was therefore important to create a sense of eager expectation and a feeling of shared commitment within my community of readers. In this case I was particularly interested in exploring the expectations that children bring to a text and how those expectations influence and sustain their subsequent engagement.

Louise Rosenblatt (1978) describes how, as a reader begins a story, she/he 'evolves certain expectations about the diction, the subject, the ideas, the themes, the kind of text that will be forthcoming . . . As the reading proceeds, attention will be fixed on the reverberations or implications that result from fulfilment or frustration of those implications.'

Rosenblatt's theory that expectation plays a key role in our enjoyment and understanding of a text was central to my investment in the project. It was this impulse of expectation that I wanted to encourage and explore before individual readings of the novel were undertaken and before the articulating of whole text responses took place. Children are often lured into tackling a challenging book if they 'catch' a teacher's enthusiasm for it and if sufficient time is taken at the point of its introduction: instilling a sense of anticipation, drawing out shared expectations, encouraging imaginative speculation are fundamental to effective teaching of the reading of literature.

Although several editions of *Bridge to Terabithia* have been published in the UK with variously 'updated' book jacket designs I felt that for this project, the original Gollancz hardback (1978), with its enigmatic front cover by Stuart Hughes and Donna Diamond's graphic black and white text illustrations would serve us best.

Katherine Paterson (1984) herself talks about fiction as being 'incarnational'. She explains that 'somehow the word or the idea has taken on flesh, has become physical, actual, real'. Her aim as a novelist is, she explains, to forge 'a deep underground connection with the reader'. Working alongside this responsive group of children I discovered how deep that connection can be.

First encounters with the book

On first encountering the book the children were simply shown an overhead transparency of the front cover. It depicts two children, one sitting, one arms raised and kneeling. Behind them towers a forest of pine trees. Between the tall, dark trunks glimpses of blue sky can be seen.

I asked my expectant readers to note the title of the novel and to remember that titles are chosen to give clues to a book's content. When they had absorbed the impact of the front cover I asked the class to record their thoughts in writing in the form of a short responsive sentence. Maybe, I suggested, they would ask a question of the book or perhaps simply note down an initial impression. A selection of their comments below suggests that Paterson's title and Hughes' illustration had effectively ignited early expectations:

This is going to be a serious book because of the dark front cover.

The silhouetted trees against the magical blue sky has a message.

This book is about travelling through difficulties.

It's a serious book with a hidden message.

It sounds like a grown up book.

Do the dark trees and the distant light mean anything?

The book is about a child who thinks that he or she has special powers that allow him or her to link one land with another.

It's about two separate people who try to overcome religion or war and try to bridge gaps between them with their feelings or personalities.

Bridge means a border.

One child is asking for help because he can see no light ahead but I think this book will be about light.

Where is the bridge ?

Who are the boys?

These responses also indicate that the children were familiar with the layered possibilities of figurative language. At this initial stage, they were simply 'reading' an illustration and responding to the three title words but their inherent creative and interpretive skills were alerted by the evocative light/dark appeal of the cover and by the seduction of the 'bridge' metaphor.

Encouraging children to read beyond the literal is essential if they are to learn how to 'interrogate' texts and to develop literary competencies. In explaining the structure and function of narrative Ted Hughes (1978) refers to story as 'a kit' which contains: 'two separable elements: its pattern and its images . . . The roads they travel on are determined by the brain's fundamental genius for metaphor. Automatically it uses the pattern of one set of images to organise quite a different set.'

Throughout their initial exposure to this novel the children were 'realising' Hughes' definition of story: they were extending literary competencies, using prior knowledge acquired from stories and from booktalk discussion to find narrative patterns, to 'read' images, to construct meaning from the limited information they were given.

Paterson characteristically reveals hints of narrative content in the titles she gives to each of her 13 chapters. I chose to capitalise on that by giving each child a list of chapter titles:

One	Jesse Oliver Aarons, Jr.
Two	Leslie Burke
Three	The Fastest Kid in the Fifth Grade
Four	Rulers of Terabithia
Five	The Giant Killers
Six	The Coming of Prince Terrien
Seven	The Golden Room
Eight	Easter
Nine	The Evil Spell

Ten	The Perfect Day
Eleven	No!
Twelve	Stranded
Thirteen	Building the Bridge

and asking him or her to record an instinctive and off-the-cuff response to each chapter title. Interestingly, in responding to the early chapters, the children did indeed confine their written recordings to one or two word comments, seemingly unrelated to the front cover. Sometimes Paterson's headings prompted questions (e.g. Who are these children? Where is Terabithia? Which one is Leslie?), sometimes observations (e.g. He's like the boy in the Machine Gunners. He looks clever. He sounds spoilt.) and in many cases (notably the title of chapter six with its Narnia resonances and chapter five with its fairy tale suggestion), encouraged strong intertextual connections. The children clearly identified Paterson's themes of fantasy and her allusions to other literature within this realistic novel. But intriguingly, as they moved through their responses to the chapter titles and arrived at the thirteenth, 'Building the Bridge', with its unmistakable reference to the novel's title, the children seemed to be searching for patterns of connection and meaning based around the book's central metaphor. Their responses became interpretive and reflective:

bridge of freedom

building relationships

re-building

a bridge for escape

new ways of living

a dream of friendship

this is about emotions

a hard chapter

making the bridge to Terabithia

At this stage I made overhead transparencies of eight illustrations and gradually, one by one, showed them to the class, linking each plate to its accompanying chapter. This new information brought about lively responses in the children and a selection of their comments exemplify Rosenblatt's theory that throughout the reading process there is constant interplay between what we expect to happen and what actually happens: reader expectations, as shown here, are both 'fulfilled and frustrated' as reading proceeds:

The pictures change everything. I think there is a message here.

I have the idea that the children are the rulers and the dog is the prince.

I've now seen the pictures and my mind is a blur.

I have a new idea about the book. I want to read it.

I like this book and want to know more.

The pictures make me feel different. They are so dramatic.

I would love to read this book.

It's a very strange type of fantasy story.

It would be great to have a dog like Prince Terrien.

The pictures mystify me.

The pictures are telling me the story.

The picture in the chapter No! is very significant for me.

This book is worrying me.

The pictures change every single chapter.

Finally, I read to the class the sensitively compiled jacket blurb (which does not reveal the central drama of the novel), the brief biographical author details and Katherine Paterson's frontispiece dedication to her son. By this stage I knew that these children were hooked on their own readings of this, as yet unread, novel. Armed with front cover, chapter titles, illustrations, story synopsis, author details and a simple but, so far, unexplained dedication inscription, each child was eager to record his or her immediate responses – in effect, to construct their own 'inner novel' within this novel. Some expectations are startlingly prophetic in terms of Paterson's narrative; some wildly imaginative but all these written responses reveal an awareness of narrative conventions, the creative possibilities of fiction and the ways in which readers bring 'world to text' – how they read in the light of their own experience of life and literary experience.

The story is about two people living in their own world of Terabithia. Jesse and Leslie become too involved with Terabithia. Prince Terrien helps Jesse to cope with a hazard that weakens his will to defend the bridge.

The writer's background is in this book.

It's about a boy and girl who make friends and one of them has an accident like falling down a pit or grows younger and they have to get to Terabithia to get her better.

I think the book is about forming of a special relationship between two people that brings them to an understanding of life and what it has in store for them.

The tragedy is that someone dies and the other has to carry on with life.

Leslie gives something important to Jesse and then she dies.

Katherine Paterson must have had a lot of good will to write a book like this and I think that being a Christian must have helped her. I would like to read this book.

I think that the bridge is not a bridge you walk over. I think it's a bridge one child has to make in his mind in order to get over a death.

I think the story is about possibility. When it says 'The Perfect Day' everything is going fine and when it says 'No!' someone dies. 'Stranded' is about how someone is left alone feeling helpless without some other person.

Expectations aroused, the children were now eager to read the novel. I bought a dozen copies of the paperback version for sharing among the class. Several children bought their own copies. Competent readers were paired with those less experienced and the goal, once everyone had read the novel, was to come together as a class for what appeared to be an ambitious booktalk session timetabled to coincide with Book Week and a parents' open day.

Articulating response and much more

We chose the school library room as our venue and, pushing the tables into the centre, sat in our huge circle of 35 readers. Every child had recently read or had *Bridge to Terabithia* read to them by another child. I told the children the story of how Katherine Paterson came to write the novel and read them brief extracts from her Newbery Acceptance speech. Then the children began to talk. For two hours as parents gathered to listen around the outside edge of the room, their children talked with assurance and touching insight about the plot, the characters, the emotional and cerebral impact of the book, the oppositional tensions and the layered quality of Paterson's writing. They shared intimate reponses and negotiated possible meanings. One child spoke of his identification with Jesse's grief and how the book had helped him come to terms with a personal loss. Another, clearly affected by the power of Paterson's language, left the group in order to compose herself before reading aloud a moving extract she wanted to explain to us. Another child spoke of how Leslie wore a plain, flower-sprigged cotton shirt 'because she was a private and honest person' whilst Jesse's two worldly sisters wore transparent blouses because 'Katherine Paterson wanted to show that they were transparent, see-through people'. Two children spoke of their experience of reading as a pair. The children's responses revealed their often sophisticated grasp of how deep structural devices in a novel operate – of how this novel turns full circle and of how Jesse grows in stature and confidence as the book proceeds.

What we all – children, teacher, parents – experienced that afternoon was a unique and affirming happening in which the imaginative power of story and the sharing of creative responses united our classroom community and established deep bonds of remembrance. I was reminded of Jerome Bruner's (1986) ideas about the richness of such learning:

> Most learning in most settings is a communal activity, a sharing of the culture. It is not just that the child must make his knowledge his own but that he must make it his own in a community of those who share his sense of belonging to a culture. It is this that

leads me to emphasise not only discovery and invention but the importance of negoti-ating and sharing . . . en route to becoming a member of the adult society.

By understanding some of the ways in which readers bring meaning to literature we as teachers and educators can promote strategies that develop literary competencies. In so doing we are helping children to 'become literary readers' (Chambers 1993) and to find the 'order and meaning' that a novelist such as Katherine Paterson has woven into her stories.

References

Bruner, J. (1986) *Actual Minds, Possible Worlds*. Harvard University Press.

Chambers, A. (1993) 'The Difference of Literature: Writing Now for the Future of Young Readers', *Children's Literature in Education*, 24 (1) (Human Sciences Press Inc., New York).

Chambers, A. (2001) *Tell Me: Children Reading and Talk*. Stroud: Thimble Press.

Culler, J. (1975) *Structuralist Poetics: Structuralism, Linguistics, and the Study of Literature*. London: Routledge and Kegan Paul.

DfEE (1998) *National Literacy Strategy Framework for Teaching*. London: DfEE.

Harding, D. W. (1977) 'Ways forward for the teacher (2): making way for the child's own "feeling comprehension" in Meek, M. *et al.* (eds) *The Cool Web*. London: Bodley Head.

Hughes, T. (1978) 'Myth and Education' in Fox, G. *et al.* (eds) *Writers Critics Children*. London: Heinemann.

Paterson, K. (1978) *Bridge to Terabithia*. London: Victor Gollancz.

Paterson, K. (1984) 'Where is Terabithia?', *Children's Literature Association Quarterly*, 9, Winter 1984/5.

Paterson, K. (1989) 'Sounds in the Heart' in *The Spying Heart*. New York: Lodestar Books, E. P. Dutton.

Rosenblatt, L. M. (1978) *The Reader, the Text, the Poem: The Transactional Theory of the Literary Work*. Carbondale and Edwardsville: Southern Illinois University Press.

Stott, J. C. (1994) 'Making Stories Mean; Making Meaning from stories: The Value of Literature for Children', *Children's Literature in Education*, 25 (4). (Human Sciences Press, Inc., New York).

Chapter 8

What could happen next? The potential of the talking book

Ruth Wood

Technology, pedagogy and creativity

Recent educational initiatives and government policies have begun to highlight what have been often neglected issues associated with the education of the nation's children. Chief among these have been issues associated with the development of thinking skills and, in particular, the notion of 'creativity' as part of the thinking process. This reviving of interest in these areas has happily coincided with the increasing use of, and skill acquisition in, the area of information and communication technology (ICT) within and across the curriculum. It is therefore opportune to consider the ways in which our children's creative thinking capacities can be enhanced, developed and extended through the use of some of the more easily accessible aspects of ICT.

The notion of developing the creative skills and capacities of individual has benefits that extend into all domains of society – the economic, political, social, technological and personal. All teachers would subscribe to this view, but they might also give pause when thinking of the requirements demanded by public examinations, league tables and other 'objective' evaluations of student attainment as to how this aspect of intellectual development can be managed. Thus, issues associated with developing the thinking and creative capacities of our school pupils are beset by three major issues:

- Do we know what we mean when we talk about developing creative thinking?

And if we do:

- How can we do this within the structures of the existing curriculum?
- How can this be evidenced through the medium of verbal/literate action which is still the main medium of assessment?

Following the original work of Guilford (1968) on creativity and the notion of divergent thinking and the work of Montgomery (1996) with able children many different ideas have been posited about creativity and creative thinking. All agree however that this is an elusive concept (Craft 2001: 13) and that generally speaking, discussions in this area are inconclusive and overlap with so many other areas of individual action (e.g. originality/ingenuity/talent) that it is not surprising that many teachers have focused on the more definable areas of their teaching. Craft suggests that insight and 'possibility thinking' lie at the 'core of imaginative activity' (Craft 2000: 3) and, as such, are activities which all of us have opportunity to engage with on a regular basis. Whenever we are presented with a problem to solve, we may apply insight alongside 'possibility thinking' in order to find a solution. In terms of information and communications technology there are many tools which allow our students and their teachers to explore some of the 'indefinables' of creativity and 'possibility thinking'. The area of ICT can prove to be a happy hunting ground for the student whose thinking does not always conform to the cultural norms of convergent thinking and 'right' answers.

In particular the area of ICT provides a particular cornucopia for those teachers for whom the developing of student literacy is a major concern. One of the more popular aspects of ICT literacy which has engaged the imagination of both lay people and educationalists alike, has been the development of software for both home and school use which can be loosely grouped under the heading of 'multimedia' technology. Here there is a broad continuum of possibility – with children using software that has been commercially produced (e.g. talking book software) to interact and engage with the material that has already been pre-defined by its authors – through to the hardware and software which allow children to define their own creative parameters of activity and to develop their own creative products.

The quality of learning experience that our children acquire through the use of software resources will be strongly affected by the design of the original material. In effect it is not a case of what the technology *can do* but what the technology can do that will *support* and *enhance* learning effectiveness. Teachers and students alike therefore are in a position to see creative thinking as occupying several different levels beginning with the design of the software (either through their own actions or those of others) through to the output generated by the teacher or the student through the use of unmodified software. Between the two are the important issues of *context* and *purpose* which in general terms are more usually designed and managed by the teacher operating within the context of the software designer.

When all these elements are taken together, teachers may be forgiven for thinking that once again they are expected to deal with the formidable task of enhancing student creative thinking skills – particularly within the area of literacy – while having to deal with a limited and unyielding system of producing 'literacy outcomes'. The rapid development of multimedia technology and its user-friendly approach has opened a whole new raft of opportunities for teachers and students, and perhaps more importantly a whole new set of ideas about creativity and literacy.

The picture book perspective

In our society, the process of developing literate individuals has focused on the ability of the individual to decode text through a process referred to as 'reading', in addition to creating written text of their own through 'writing' – something which Papert (1993: 11) referred to as 'letteracy'. In the early years of a child's education, pictures are generally used to support this process; helping the reader to translate the written word into meaning and recognise that text in this format can represent spoken language. Illustrated books, which are designed for this very reason, have been available for many years with something resembling the modern picture book emerging in the late nineteenth century (Lewis 2001: xvi). Since the 1980s, the sophistication of picture books has increased dramatically with author/illustrators creating complex and challenging texts for both adults and children alike. These texts combine writing and illustrations creatively, for example Anthony Browne's *The Tunnel* (1989) and *Voices in the Park* (1998) as well as author John Marsden and illustrator Shaun Tan, *The Rabbits* (2001) to name but a few. The pictures themselves are works of art and the reader is encouraged to linger over each, exploring the visual element more closely in order to interpret what has been presented. The creative energy which is evident in such picture books lies not with the illustrations alone however, it is the way written text and the picture as text work together, what Lewis (2001: 36) refers to as the 'mutual interanimation'. Here, the reader is challenged by the interactions between the two media and is encouraged to explore the meaning that exists between their union. Both picture and text are essential and one without the other would change or diminish the overall experience of the reader if not change the story entirely. Because the traditional role of pictures within books has generally been to provide the reader with visual cues which have supported the process of decoding written text, picture books seem to be viewed as appropriate for young children or for those who face difficulty in learning to read. Contemporary picture books can challenge more able readers, including adults. Consider works of art such as *The Ambassadors* by Holbein or the *Mona Lisa* by Leonardo Da Vinci. Interpretations, particularly for the latter example, have been offered, considered and discussed for many years and still no one is able to agree. In all of these instances, the person attempting to interpret the painting has been 'reading' visual texts. Picture books have much to offer yet the focus within education appears to relinquish such books when a reader is considered to be proficient in decoding written text. A review offered by one individual on *The Rabbits*, written by John Marsden and illustrated by Shaun Tan, provided an interesting insight into the way picture books appeal to a wide range of ages and abilities:

> The story is a deep metaphor for the colonisation of Australia (at least that is this adult's interpretation – I know children as young as 5 who have found their own meanings). The consistent and beautiful world of the narrators gives way to the mad (and bitter-sweet comical) technology of the incoming rabbits.

As an arts-in-education professional I find this book works as a piece of art more than any other I know – you can interrogate it, build meaning, and combine it with your own experience of the world. It does not preach and has an open ending that begs 'what if?' questions... It is both very simple and very rich at the same time.

(accessed on www.amazon.co.uk June 2003)

New literacies and multimedia storybooks

Recently, there has been increased interest in visual literacy and media literacy (DfES 2002) and the ways in which meaning can be conveyed through pictures, animation, sound, video in addition to, or instead of, written text. With the advent of technology, these individual elements may be combined into a rich, multimedia experience for learners. Since the early 1990s, multimedia CD-ROMs have been developed which have, to a certain extent, brought picture books to life. Such technology has been referred to as 'talking book software'. Broderbund's Living Book series offered interactive talking books with high quality and entertaining animations activated through the click of a mouse button. Little was required in terms of information technology skills and, as such, this software was, and still is, highly accessible. Titles from the series include *Just Grandma and Me* by Mercer Mayer (1993) and *The Tortoise and the Hare* by Aesop (1993). In addition to a picture, each page provides sections of the story as written text which is highlighted as a character or narrator reads. At the same time, animations and sound are played which effectively act out the story as it is read. Once this has finished, the picture may become interactive to the reader who explores the scene with clicks of the mouse to activate animations. Such design relies on the natural curiosity of the child who will actively select parts of the scene with the hope of further rewarding animations such as dancing insects or frogs which jump from mail boxes.

Sherston have produced a number of talking books which have a limited number of interactive elements on each screen, for example Sherston's *Naughty Stories* (1994). The design, in this instance, is similar in many ways to the illustrated stories which were designed to support the development of reading skills. The pictures clearly relate to the written text and offer visual cues which support the reader in the process of decoding. Buttons at the bottom of the screen activate the animation (the eye) and narration (the ear) while arrows enable the reader to progress through the story (see Figure 8.1).

Education and entertainment have been fused into resources such as talking books and is now commonly referred to as 'edutainment'. In some instances, the edutainment appears to lead in a different direction to the story. Even though such instances may have educational value such as the development of anticipation and prediction skills (Fox 2002: 146), it has been questioned whether they actually enhance the story or instead, are incidental and perhaps serve to detract from it (Davies and O'Sullivan,

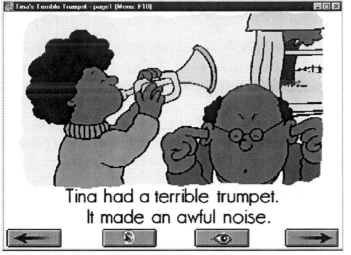

Tina had a terrible trumpet.
It made an awful noise.

FIGURE 8.1 *Naughty Stories*, CD-ROM, Sherston

2002: 107). As pointed out by Burrell and Trushell (1997: 3) the first screen in *The Tortoise and the Hare* has a total of 24 interactive elements or 'hotspots' activated by mouse clicks. Seven of these were considered by the researchers as being supplemental to the story while the remaining 17 were considered to be incidental. The difference in the number of supplemental and incidental elements is evident throughout the story. Although children enjoy activating hotspots on each page in order to observe the effects, it is not always possible to read the entire story. Due to the number of interactive features, children may spend a great deal of time activating the hotspots rather than progressing through the story. The implications are that the children are perhaps interacting with the technology rather than with the story itself.

While observing children interacting with such software, their discussions concerning what should be explored and their responses once they have activated the selected hotspot clearly indicated that children generally enjoy such experiences. Additionally, the discussion arising from the exploration of the on-screen story is a rich opportunity for speaking and listening; an essential part of language acquisition and development. Research often makes reference to the motivational nature of information and communications technology and talking books are no exception (Collins *et al.* 1997, Adam and Wild 1997). The potential for multimedia to support and enhance the development of children's reading is evident in the attraction such a 'book' holds to children of all ages and abilities. It tends to follow that if children are interested and motivated, the likelihood that they will engage with the task presented is increased. This in turn will increase the potential for learning. However, if the design of the software is such that the thinking has been completed for the children, children effectively act as consumers of multimedia and the opportunities for 'possibility thinking' are diminished.

Current use of talking book software

A recent survey conducted by the Books Alive Project Team (Wood *et al.* 2003) found that Sherston talking books and those created by Broderbund were used most frequently in primary and nursery schools. More specifically, Key Stage 1 and nurseries accounted for approximately 90 per cent of the schools who used the software. More interestingly, there are indications that approximately three in every four teachers are aware of the existence of such software and one in every two teachers makes use of talking books within the classroom. Generally, the software was used to support word recognition, sound/symbol correspondence and the development of basic reading skills. Teachers indicated that the reason for using such software was because of its ability to increase motivation through fun and entertainment. Teachers who employed the use of talking books in Key Stage 2 explained that such resources were used with children who experienced difficulties in reading or who were reluctant to read. In a sense, contemporary picture books and talking book software are perceived in the same way – as appropriate for young readers who are developing their reading skills rather than for competent or able readers.

From paper to screen

Talking books such as those first created by Broderbund were, in some ways, ahead of their time. The rich combination of sound, picture animation and written text offered a unique learning opportunity which brought educational technology into a new era. From their introduction in the early 1990s, little change has occurred in their design and, in the light of contemporary picture books currently available and technological developments, it is probably an appropriate time to consider how this resource should move forward. Features which allow children to explore the story, view specific incidents from an alternative viewpoint and move within and between scenes may be supported by carefully constructed multimedia content. Hyperlinks would allow movement in a non-linear fashion and opportunities for selecting alternative journeys through a text may therefore be possible, offering the reader an active role in the development of the story. Current design and use of talking books needs to be reassessed, particularly when technology has reached a stage where adventure games consist of visual text with plots which have the potential to challenge children's imagination and understanding so effectively. The relatively well known slogan 'if you've read the book, see the film' seems to apply to the development of multimedia talking books. At present, existing stories are transferred to the on-screen format and this process in itself limits the effectiveness of the design. For example, real books tend to be linear and the pages are rarely the same size as the screen. The authors and illustrators will have designed content based upon the requirements of a paper-based medium. Instead of beginning with the paper-based source, imagine the possibilities of starting at the screen. Difficulties in transferring from one medium to another will always exist and there are strengths and weaknesses for each. However, with the advent of computers held in the palm of a hand, the potential of highly portable electronic books commonly referred to as e-books, is already a reality.

Creative communication

Creativity in design of software such as talking books should, perhaps, be accompanied by opportunities for children to communicate in an equally creative manner. If the word processor allowed us to become authors and the photocopier enabled us to become publishers, video cameras took us one step closer to directing and editing our own films. The advances of digital video cameras have made such roles even more accessible. Effectively, the possibility of communicating in a variety of formats with a range of media has never been greater. As designers and developers of multimedia, children are in control of their own knowledge development and may explore a vast range of possibilities which present their thoughts and ideas in various formats. The potential for learning may be enhanced through occupying the role of the creator rather than the consumer (Jonassen 2000: 206).

Multimedia communication in itself is nothing new – we live in a multimedia world so we are constantly communicating with each other through varied combinations of visual images, sounds, movement and text. Digital cameras capture images which can be transferred to a computer quickly and easily. Images can be selected for use or they can be deleted and retaken. This speed is a great advantage as pictures can be used to immediate effect, providing almost instantaneous feedback.

Creating an image or a sequence of images which tell a story can be an excellent starting point for children. In a similar way to talking books, discussion can provide a rich context for the development of language; by considering and discussing the composition of a picture, children articulate their ideas and engage with the subject matter. This, in turn may support their ability to translate ideas into written format. Additionally, linking pictures together using multimedia authoring software could create a simple yet highly effective multimedia storybook. Figure 8.2 illustrates how stories are generally constructed – a linear format which is often simulated in talking book software.

FIGURE 8.2

Multimedia authoring software such as PowerPoint (Microsoft) or Hyperstudio (Richard Wagner Publishing Company) provide opportunities for the author to explore a non-linear format where the sequence in which the screens are viewed can be determined by the reader (see Figure 8.4). This is achieved through the use of hyperlinks which effectively connect screens together. The reader would activate hyperlinks by selecting a button or hotspot with a mouse click. Clearly, the routes through the story will be limited to those created by the author but for both reader and author, the opportunities for exploring alternative story structures is a reality. In addition to this, sound, written text as well as visual images (both still and moving) can be included and activated through the use of hotspots. This approach may encourage a more creative approach to story writing which would appeal to a child living in a technologically rich society.

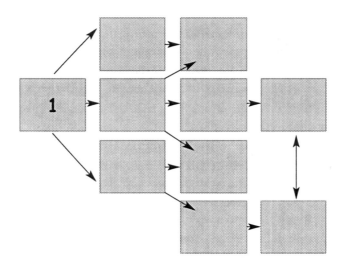

FIGURE 8.3

As designer, author and illustrator, children creating a multimedia storybook would need to make decisions regarding both choice of media and hyperlinks available. These decisions would affect the impact the story would have upon the reader. For example, alternative journeys through a story would provide opportunities for the reader to explore a specific character perhaps, or a setting. Sub-plots and decision-making, which determine how conflict is resolved and endings achieved, could be designed as part of the story structure.

Effectively, the organisation of the system has infinite possibilities and can be as limited or as open as required. To help children develop their skills, knowledge and understanding as multimedia developers and storytellers, it would be necessary to offer some guidance in the design process. Because multimedia projects can be so open ended, it is important to design something which is manageable and achievable from the onset. This may appear to be a contradiction, but it is still possible to respond creatively within a clearly defined and manageable project outline. Additionally, it may be possible to develop the project further once the initial design has been completed – for example additional sub-plots may be added to a story once the main strands have been created. Careful consideration of the multimedia elements needs to be encouraged so that children include such features to achieve a specific purpose. If sound would add atmosphere and therefore enhance the reader's experience it would be an appropriate addition to a setting. Getting the balance right between the range of media is also part of the design process. If one element should dominate it could detract from the story. Designs would need navigational cues so that the reader is able to move between screens with relative ease. Buttons which are too small or difficult to find only serve to frustrate the reader! A storyboard would provide an extremely useful overview which clearly maps out the various routes alongside the media content for each screen. Here, programs such as *Kidspiration* (Inspiration Software Inc) would enable the designer to plan the possible routes and change the outline easily. Aesthetics such as colour combination and screen layout are equally essential. If the screen is appealing and attractive, the reader will be more comfortable with its use. Finally, as a designer it is difficult to test the result objectively. It is important to test it on other individuals to ensure navigation, content and appearance are as effective as possible.

As designers, children will explore the structure and the content of stories through a rich learning experience. Characters, settings and plot are all central to the development of a multimedia story and the rationale behind the choice of media is central to the child's understanding of the story from the perspective of both author and reader. Whilst participating in such activities, children become more aware of the way multimedia materials work and can become critical of the design of existing examples. The post-modern child experiences multimedia on a daily basis. Telling a story with multimedia is a further dimension that has much to offer. Children need to be more than 'letterate' and through such opportunities, creativity is offered another avenue where 'possibility thinking' and 'imaginative activity' can develop.

References

Adam, N. and Wild, M. (1997) 'Applying CD-ROM interactive storybooks to learning to read', *Journal of Computer Assisted Learning*, 13, 119–32.

Browne, A. (1997) *The Tunnel*. London: Walker Books.

Browne, A. (1998) *Voices in the Park*. London: Transworld Children's Books.

Burrell, C. and Trushell, J. (1997) 'Eye-candy' in 'interactive books' – a wholesome diet?, *Reading*, 31 (2), 3–6.

Collins, J., Hammond, M. and Wellington, J. (1997) *Teaching and Learning with Multimedia*. London: Routledge.

Craft, A. (2000) *Creativity across the Primary Curriculum: framing and developing practice*. London: Routledge.

Craft, A. (2001) An Analysis of Research and Literature on Creativity in Education, QCA http://www.ncaction.org.uk/creativity/creativity_report.pdf (accessed July 2003).

Davies, H. and O'Sullivan, O. (2002) 'Literacy and ICT in the Primary Classroom: The Role of the Teacher' in Loveless, A. and Dore, B. (eds) *ICT in the Primary School*, pp. 102–24. Buckingham: Open University Press.

DfES (2002) *Transforming the Way We Learn*. HMSO.

Fox, B. (2002) 'Talking Stories, Textoids and Dialogic Reading' in Monteith, M. (ed.) *Teaching Primary Literacy With ICT*, pp. 144–57. Buckingham: Open University Press.

Guilford, J. P. (1968) *Intelligence, Creativity and their Educational Implications*. San Diego, Calif.: Knapp.

Jonassen, D. H. (2000) *Computers as Mindtools: Engaging Critical Thinking*, 2nd edn. New Jersey: Merrill.

Lewis, D. (2001) *Reading Contemporary Picturebooks*. London: Routledge Falmer.

Marsden, J. and Tan, S. (illustrator) (2001) *The Rabbits*. Melbourne: Lothian Books.

Montgomery, D. (1996) *Educating the Able*. London: Cassell.

Papert, S. (1993) *The Children's Machine*. New York: Basic Books.

Wood, R., Rawlings, A. and Ozturk, A. (2003) 'Towards a New Understanding: The Books Alive Multimedia Project', *Reading* 37 (2), 90–3.

Discography/software

Hyperstudio, Richard Wagner Publishing Company.

Just Grandma and Me (1993) SSCV/Broderbund Living Books.

Kidspiration, Inspiration Software, Inc. 7412 SW Beaverton-Hillsdale Hwy Suite 102, Portland.

The Tortoise and the Hare (1993) Random House/Broderbund Living Books.

Sherston's *Naughty Stories*, CD-ROM (1994) Wiltshire, Sherston Software.

PowerPoint, Microsoft Corporation.

Chapter 9

Closely observed poems

Michael Lockwood

Introduction

Creative writers have been telling us for a number of years now that we have taken a wrong turning in the way we are currently approaching writing in school. David Almond in his Carnegie Medal acceptance speech in 1999 warned against the 'noses-to-the-grindstone treadmill kind of work...that is observable, recordable and well-nigh constant' and pleaded for 'moments when children must be left alone, given space and silence and respect' (Almond 1999). Philip Pullman has echoed this, pointing out forcefully that writing does not happen in the way the National Literacy Strategy (NLS) suggests it should, and recalling, by contrast, times as a teacher when 'a child in my class discovered that he or she could take time and write something true and meaningful' (Pullman 2003: 11). Most recently, the Children's Laureate, Michael Morpurgo, has taken the Year 6 SATs writing tests himself to highlight what he feels is the impossibility of 'completing a story to order in exam conditions' (Neill 2003: 10).

The comments of these professional writers suggest that in reforming the teaching of writing through the NLS we may well have thrown out the creative baby with the bathwater of discredited teaching approaches. The genre-based approach to writing developed in Australia in the 1980s and 1990s, and characterised by Pullman as 'before you write a story, you have to make a class list of "the features of a good story opening"' (Pullman 2003: 11), has had a strong influence on the NLS writing objectives in the *Framework for Teaching* (DfES 1998). While no-one suggests a return to the unregulated English curriculum of the 1960s and 1970s, and while it still needs to be recognised that for most children 'the act of writing is less about an artistic encounter and more about a practical and rather complicated process of construction' (Hiatt and Rooke 2002: 1), it seems clear that the rigorous genre-based approach currently holding sway needs to be modified by a recognition that children need time and space in an overcrowded curriculum to develop personal creativity in writing. The signs are that the warnings from writers and from teachers have been heard, at least partially, by the DfES. Their latest strategy document, *Excellence and Enjoyment*, states: 'As well as giving them the essential tools for learning, primary education is about children experiencing the joy of discovery, solving problems, being creative in writing, art, music...' and teachers are referred to some materials from a QCA project, *Creativity: Find it, promote it*, available on the QCA website at www.ncaction.org.uk (DfES 2003: 4, 31). However, the TES's headline reporting on *Excellence and Enjoyment* suggests how the argument has not yet been completely won: 'Ministers refuse to abolish SATs but promise more creativity' (Ward 2003: 1).

In addition to the voices of professional writers, cognitive psychologists such as Howard Gardner have been telling us over the past two decades of increasing evidence that children have widely different learning styles. We now have a clearer view of 'the plurality of intellect': that we all make use, to differing degrees, of at least seven kinds of intelligence, and that for many individuals the linguistic and logical-mathematical intelligences which dominate school curricula are not the favoured way of thinking and learning. For many, the balance of their multiple intelligences favours spatial, musical, bodily-kinaesthetic, interpersonal or intrapersonal thinking and learning (Gardner 1993: 8–9). It follows that a narrow approach to writing in the classroom, which presents opportunities for children to use only some of their 'rainbow' of intelligences, to use Sue Teele's metaphor for our unique, individual blends of Gardner's seven primary intelligences (Teele 2000: vii), will seriously disadvantage many children and not bring out the full potential in most.

Poetry has always been at the heart of debates over approaches to teaching writing. The growing calls for greater time and space for creativity in writing recall the work of two important figures from the 1960s and 1970s, Ted Hughes, poet, and Jill Pirrie, poetry teacher. Though they both championed creativity in this period, neither could be further from the traditional caricature of the 'creative writing' teacher. Both Hughes and Pirrie used and wrote about a disciplined, structured and quite formal approach to poetry writing, which certainly did not involve setting fire to wastepaper baskets or blowing bubbles! On the other hand, neither approached writing poems by listing the features required and checking that they were all present in the finished poem. In the current situation, there are elements in the approach to writing suggested by Hughes and Pirrie which need to be rediscovered, and this is what the poetry project described below tried to do.

The background

The poetry writing activities described here had their initial inspiration in the work of Ted Hughes. In 1967 Hughes published *Poetry in the Making*, based on a series of radio programmes he wrote for BBC Schools Broadcasting. In the book, Hughes not only talks revealingly about his own poetry but puts forwards his views on how poetry writing should be approached in schools. He proceeds from the assumption that:

by showing to a pupil's imagination many opportunities and few restraints, and instilling into him[/her] confidence and a natural motive for writing, the odds are that something – maybe not much, but something – of our common genius will begin to put a word in.

(Hughes 1967: 12)

Hughes suggests strategies to use in the classroom to provide these imaginative opportunities, such as 'learning to think', which involves focused concentration on a small simple object and at the same time 'full-out descriptive writing, to a set length, in a set time, in a loose verse form' (p. 64). Any object will do, or the subject could be an animal you want to 'capture' in words, Hughes suggests, and five minutes or ten minutes at a time can be long enough. Using artificial limits such as a time constraint, or having to put each phrase on a fresh line, 'rouses the brain's resources . . . [and] many things that are usually hidden find themselves rushed into the open' (p. 23).

Hughes' approach was developed in the classroom by Jill Pirrie, as she describes in her later book *On Common Ground* (1987). Hughes says in his introduction that Pirrie's unique achievement as a teacher was to be able to unearth 'latent talent' for writing poetry in 'an average class, from ordinary pupils' (Pirrie 1987: viii). Pirrie's classes at Halesworth Middle School in Suffolk were even more inclusive than the current literacy hour is intended to be: they were mixed ability and Pirrie found that the 'common ground' of poetry, like Hughes' 'common genius', had as much to offer the less able as the more able (Pirrie 1987: 80). Hughes refers to poems containing 'minutely detailed observations' as 'the five finger exercises of Jill Pirrie's method', but he points out that in the most fully developed of the children's poems, 'meticulous objectivity is opened to psychological depth and to subjective vitality (Pirrie 1987: x). As Pirrie wrote in the second anthology of her pupils' work, *Apple Fire*: 'In poetry, children find the detachment which confronts reality and refuses to compromise the facts. Therein lies the integrity which is the hallmark of both the poet and the scientist' (Pirrie 1993: 22).

The poetry writing project described here was not meant to be a simple return to a form of 1960s, hit-or-miss 'creative writing'. As well as making links with other creative disciplines, such as art, the intention was to show the links between poetry and other areas of the curriculum, particularly environmental science. One aim was certainly to suggest that poetry's place in the curriculum was not as limited as often thought and that poetry could provide a way of observing, thinking and learning in other subject areas. This involved challenging the conventional view both of what poetry is and does and how we think and learn in other areas of the curriculum. As Karl Popper has said, 'The scientist and the artist . . . are both trying to extend our knowledge and experience by the use of creative imagination subjected to critical control' (in McGee 1973: 68). To this can be added Myra Barrs and Sue Ellis's claim that: 'Poems offer a special way of thinking. They can express some of the more intuitive, affective aspects of our perceptions, those which are sometimes left out of a narrowly conceived, cognitively orientated curriculum' (Barrs and Ellis 1995: 22).

The Poetry Project

The project was carried out with Year 6 pupils in a middle school over several weeks of the summer term. Although not designed to fit in with the NLS Framework, the writing certainly contributed towards meeting objective T13: 'to write a sequence of poems linked by theme or form'. In this case, the theme was Close-Ups, both close observation of what was being looked at or remembered, and careful observation of our own responses to it. The children individually and in pairs produced several poems linked in this way and these built up into a class sequence.

Choosing what to observe

The children sometimes worked from an actual object which they brought in or which I supplied. Objects such as stones, flowers, leaves and feathers could be looked at closely using hand lenses and then sketched as part of work in art using various media such as charcoal, ink or caran d'ache. This encouraged still-life observation of the objects, looking at them from a variety of angles and in different light, turning them over and feeling their surface texture. Time and space was allowed for this important stage.

When I wanted the children to look at living creatures, I used photographs taken from commercial poster packs. These were marvellous full colour, magnified scientific stills of a variety of wildlife, where part of the effort of attention was already done for us through the work of the camera. I hoped these would help to produce what Ted Hughes called descriptions which are 'detailed, scientific in their objectivity and microscopic attentiveness' (Hughes 1967: 64). Creatures to be observed were carefully selected and anything cuddly or cute (squirrels, rabbits, cats, etc.) was banned as likely to bring too many stereotyped responses and clichéd descriptions with it. Insects, spiders and other distinctly uncuddly creepy crawlies often made the best subjects precisely because the detailed photographs showed them in a new light and prejudices had to be overcome. Photographs which produced the best close observation came from Philip Green Educational packs with titles such as 'Pond Life', 'Our Senses' and 'Small Creatures'.

First impressions

First of all I asked the children to take time to look very carefully at their object or photographed creature and simply jot down a list of immediate observations and responses. One pair of children produced this from a picture of a frog:

> Slipery, slimy
> Shiny, soft smooth skin
> Browney, greeney colour

Little black dots in the side
Long legs
Flat feet
Yellow, bulgy eyes
Bubbly frogspoorn in the pond

I asked more able writers to divide their list into 'what I see' and 'how I feel'. As Ted Hughes suggested, I used a time limit of five or ten minutes at this stage to galvanise attention. I chose an object too and wrote with the children. After this, the children shared their first thoughts with a trusted partner but without giving feedback. I showed my photo to the children and read out just a few of my observations, being careful not to suggest the things I listed were the 'answers'.

Using the senses

The next stage was to encourage the children to revise and extend their initial jottings by deliberately using all the senses they could. With physical objects it was possible to use touch and smell as well as sight and hearing to refine the first impressions, though taste just had to be imagined! With the photographs, this stage of observation meant imagining what the creature might sound, smell, feel and possibly even taste like. The children again shared their extended lists with partners, checking that each had used all their senses, and some were shared with the whole class, including mine.

I stressed at this stage the need for the children to keep focused on the object or photograph whilst using their other senses. I also asked the children to use what D. H. Lawrence called the sixth sense, the sense of wonder, whilst looking at their subject or object. They should imagine that they were looking at it for the first time and that it was something amazing. I told them that Lawrence also said poetry 'makes a new effort of attention, and "discovers" a new world within the known world' (Kalnins 1992).

Making comparisons

We had read poems based on close observation and the senses before starting to write ourselves and talked about how the most memorable descriptions are ones which use comparisons to help the reader visualise what is being observed. The next stage in our closely observed poetry writing was for the children to add to their list of jottings any comparisons that came to mind from looking at the object or creature. For example, one child added 'shiny wet fur looks like velvet' to her observations of a water rat, and another, looking at a highly magnified photo of a blue damselfly, thought the eyes had 'little squares like wire mesh'. The emphasis was on 'making comparisons' rather than on 'writing metaphors and similes' here. Again I wrote with the children and went through the same process.

Using information

The photo packs used contained notes to accompany the photographs, which gave scientific information about the creatures. I encouraged the children to add any of these facts which interested them to the lists they were compiling. So the child writing about the water rat added that it made squeaky noises when scared and was good at hiding, and another added that the moorhen in her photograph used crumpled up reeds to make a nest. I wanted to make it clear that we were not ignoring scientific facts about these creatures, but adding this information to what our senses and our imagination had already told us, and so building up a rounded picture in our minds using all our intelligences.

Putting it in writing

The next step was the crucial one of moving from a list of jottings to a piece of connected writing. I modelled this step for the children by demonstrating how I made my list of observations into continuous prose, ticking off items from the list as I used them, crossing out other things I decided not to use and adding in something new that only occurred to me as I was writing. My demonstration writing was about a photo of a waterflea:

> The waterflea's see-through sac floats through the dark space of the pond. The five pale-green eggs inside look like mini kiwi-fruits. Her black eyes stare out blankly onto the darkness. Her antennae are like antlers, but they're covered in fine hairs. She uses them to feel for food in the water. The dark eye and dark green spine remind me of a sea-horse, swimming soundlessly and jerkily.

The children wrote out their lists in the same way, shared the drafts, no more than a paragraph in length, with their response partners, and gave each other feedback.

Making it into a poem

The final step for these close-up poems was to move from a piece of continuous prose to a piece of free verse. Again, I modelled this process, thinking aloud about the choices I made as I decided where to begin and end a line, how to put a word at the start of a line for emphasis, how to make the poem go faster or slower by changing the line length. At this stage the focus was on arranging the lines and not on spelling, sentence structure or punctuation. We agreed to sort these out when we were happy with our poems. Rhyme was discouraged, but some children found it easier to use a simple non-rhyming structure such as a list poem or a shape poem, where the words were written inside the outline of the animal or object. Some of the children found it helped to address their poem directly to the creature or thing observed, as with the 'Mottled Moth': 'You've got markings like the patterns on carpets / But I know that if I touch you dust will come off on my hand.'

Presenting the poems

The children word-processed their poems and then edited and proof-read them on screen, working with their response partners. At the end of the project we made a display of poems with accompanying photographs and any drawings made by the children themselves. One of the poster packs we used included poems about the animals in the photographs, but the children were unanimous in preferring their own poems, so, when the display was taken down, copies of the poems were included in the poster pack for reading by other pupils in the school.

Final thoughts

Teaching literacy through creativity has benefits for teachers as well as children. Just as children develop their potential through activities which allow them to use their creative abilities, so teachers can gain personally and professionally as well. I wrote with the children throughout the project and the experience led me to continue revising my own drafts afterwards. This eventually resulted in a close observation poem inspired by a photograph, 'Pond Skaters', which I was able to publish in an anthology about Minibeasts.

The project outlined here is only one possible way to introduce creative disciplines into poetry writing. The children's poet John Foster has said that his work has three sources of inspiration: imagination, observation and experience (in Carter 2002: vii). The project tried to emphasise the first and also include the second, but it could certainly have been developed further by going on to draw more on the children's own experience. In the words of Ted Hughes quoted above, Jill Pirrie aimed in her teaching to bring her young writers to a stage where 'meticulous objectivity is opened to psychological depth and to subjective vitality', liberating in them an 'imaginative objectivity' (Pirrie 1987: x). So the children in the project could build on their discipline of close-up observation by introducing more of their own personal responses and individual impressions of the things they wrote about, and by making links with their own experiences.

To conclude, there are encouraging signs that creative approaches in writing generally are being recognised again in primary schools. A shining example is the work of Jill Hanson, Literacy Co-ordinator, and her colleagues at Binfield CE Primary, near Bracknell. Binfield has achieved Beacon School status for its development of a writing curriculum which sees each and every child as a writer, and encourages all children to see themselves as writers. In the school's CD-ROM, *Let's Write*, which Jill Hanson scripted, she speaks of putting 'some magic and excitement back into the curriculum' through creative approaches to literacy which encourage children to take risks: 'encourage them to reach for the moon and they will reach the stars'. In conversation, Jill freely admits to being a 'creative writing' teacher from an earlier age who has now found herself back in fashion. However, the good practice described on her CD-ROM, and apparent in her classroom and those of her colleagues, suggests that it *is* possible to marry the best of earlier creative writing and process writing approaches with the modelling and demonstration writing techniques of the NLS's shared and guided writing which Jill believes in passionately. Closely observing my own and the children's poems for this project leads me to the same conclusion.

References

Almond, D. (1999) Carnegie Medal acceptance speech, 14 July.

Barrs, M. and Ellis, S. (1995) *Hands On Poetry: using poetry in the classroom*. London: Centre for Language in Primary Education.

Carter, J. (2002) *Just Imagine: creative ideas for writing*. London: David Fulton Publishers.

DfES (1998) *National Literacy Strategy: Framework for Teaching*. London: DfES.

DfES (2003) *Excellence and Enjoyment*. London: DfES.

Gardner, H. (1993) *Multiple Intelligences: the theory in practice*. New York: Basic Books.

Hiatt, K. and Rooke, J. (2002) *Creativity and Writing Skills: finding a balance in the primary classroom*. London: David Fulton Publishers.

Hughes, T. (1967) *Poetry in the Making: an anthology of poems and programmes from* listening and writing. London: Faber.

Kalnins, M. (ed.) (1992) *D. H. Lawrence: Selected Poems*. London: Everyman.

McGee, B. (1973) *Popper*. London: Fontana.

Neill, H. (2003) 'Michael's Mission', *Times Educational Supplement*, 16 May.

NLS (1998) *Framework for Teaching*. London: DfES.

Pirrie, J. (1987) *On Common Ground*. London: Hodder and Stoughton.

Pirrie, J. (1993) *Apple Fire: the Halesworth Middle School anthology*. Newcastle: Bloodaxe Books.

Pullman. P. (2003) 'They're reading like robots', *The Sunday Times*, 6 April.

QCA (2003) *Creativity: find it, promote it*. www.ncaction.org.uk (accessed 4/7/03).

Teele, S. (2000) *Rainbows of Intelligence: exploring how students learn*. London: Sage.

Ward, H. (2003) 'Tests here to stay but stress will be eased', *Times Educational Supplement*, 16 April.

CD-ROM *Let's Write*, available from Jill Hanson, Binfield CE Primary, Benetfeld Road, Binfield, Bracknell, Berkshire RG42 4EW, 01344 860106 or www.binfieldschool.co.uk

Chapter 10

Drama and writing: enlivening their prose

Teresa Grainger

Drama is a valuable tool for developing children's oral and written voices. Educational classroom drama is not concerned with stories retold in action, but with the exploration and investigation of texts and the creation of alternative perspectives through the co-authorship of new and living fictions. Classroom drama, as distinct from theatre and free-flow play, occupies a central place on the drama continuum and involves the use of a range of drama conventions and teacher intervention and involvement in role. In classroom drama, also known as process drama (O'Neill 1995), children create and inhabit an imaginary world and learn from living inside this open-ended world. The National Curriculum (NC) (DfEE 1999) includes the statutory requirement to develop such drama and focuses upon discovering and shaping the unknown, rather than acting out what is already decided. Although elements of theatre will inevitably stray into the realms of classroom drama, in such drama children are not invited to act or perform, but to believe, engage and learn creatively (Craft *et al.* 2001).

The motivating power of drama can make a significant contribution to enlivening children's writing and their imaginative and emotional engagement in drama can act as a valuable precursor to shared, guided and independent writing. In the world of fiction, strong emotive texts and process drama, work as potent partners to empower writing in a range of genres. The world of non-fiction can also be brought to life and energised through dramatic activities, which seek to build understanding or represent the children's knowledge about an area of the curriculum. This too can be reflected and summarised through the accompanying writing, as the NC states: 'Drama activities can play a real part in the interrelationship between reading, writing, speaking and listening' (DfEE 1999).

Writing in role

Classroom drama offers additional lived and imagined experience which children can use as a basis for writing, either from inside the imaginary world or outside it after the drama. There are at least three kinds of writing linked to work in role:

Writing in role: writing undertaken from inside the lived experience of drama and written during the imaginative action;

Writing alongside role: writing composed from a relative distance, written after the lived experience of drama;

Writing 'as if' in role: writing composed 'as if' in role, without any experience of dramatic engagement.

Clearly the last kind of in-role work is merely nominally related to drama and is only a low level 'let's pretend' writing activity of which publishers are fond. Writing 'as if' in role misses the opportunity to interact in the world of drama prior to the writing. Genuine writing in role however, during or after some dramatic engagement, can provide a clearer than usual stance or sense of perspective. Through alignment with a particular character in a text, or the role adoption of a journalist's or police officer's perspective for example, the voice and views of the author are shaped and formed. Through this oral work the content of later writing is developed which is likely to give an edge to the composition and heighten its effect on the reader. Such writing also helps children build belief in their roles and deepen their imaginative involvement in the drama. Their empathy with the role and emotional identification with the characters may well surface in the writing, for, as Barrs and Cork (2001) found with Key Stage 2 writers, living through drama leads to strongly imagined writing in role. Their research suggests that writing in role can be a real aid to children's progress as writers, as has also been argued elsewhere (e.g. McNaughton 1997; Grainger 2001, 2003).

Writing in drama time

Drama needs to be integrated into the curriculum, since through writing in role and writing alongside role, learners can develop and articulate their voices in a wealth of cross-curricula contexts. Writing in drama time may take place in any of the three phases of the drama (Grainger and Cremin 2001).

Phase I – First encounters: Writing to create the drama context
Writing and drawing in this part of the drama can contribute to the children's sense of who they are (the people) and where they are (the place) as they build their belief in the imaginary world.

Phase II – Conflicts and tensions: Writing to open the drama out
Writing and drawing in this part of the drama draws upon and helps shape the

children's response to the central challenge (the predicament) of the drama. As they respond to the problem, their commitment deepens and they may experience the drama as real. Writing in role is often very productive at this stage.

Phase III – Resolutions: Writing to draw the drama together

Writing and drawing in this part of the drama helps children resolve the predicament, consider the issues and connect their learning to the wider world in which they live. Some of this writing may reflect upon the drama from one character's perspective or a more distant viewpoint may be adopted.

Teachers who are aware of the writing possibilities in a historical drama, for instance on Victorian England, can plan such opportunities into one or more of the phases, although it is also important to seize opportunities which avail themselves during the drama. When writing emerges as a natural response to a situation in which the children find themselves, then its authenticity increases, and its audience and purpose are clear. For example, at the close of a drama session in which a class of six-year-olds had travelled on their magic carpet to visit Rainbow Island, the children expressed the desire to visit their friends, the Rainbow Fairies again, and suggested that they could write to them. Their teacher, eager to capitalise on this interest, encouraged them to do so and found some of the least able writers in her class put pencil to paper with a remarkable degree of commitment, energy and enthusiasm. Both Ben and Jonathon's writing reflect their involvement in the Rainbow Fairies' predicament, which was that the bad weather threatened their existence, since they needed a balance of sun and rain to survive. Jonathon, normally a very reluctant writer, was on Stage 3 of the Special Needs Register for attention deficit, yet he knew exactly what he wanted to say to the Rainbow Fairies.

If it happens
again, use
that idea
or you will
all drown.

Use water from
the bottle.

In the drama, Jonathon was unusually involved, enthralled by the fiction which he and his class created and he contributed the idea of using a bottle of water 'as tall as a hall' to give the Rainbow Fairies their homes back. The drama had enabled him to generate and share ideas, and in his writing he was able to voice one of these ideas with conviction. Following the drama, Jonathon and his class also enjoyed reading tales about other kinds of fairy folk, as invented and unique as the Rainbow Fairies themselves.

A contrasting Key Stage 2 example involved a geography session during a unit of work on the environment. The book *Giant* by Juliet and Charles Snape was being used, and during the 'conflicts and tension' phase of the drama (Grainger and Cremin 2001), the children created TV news items about the strange disappearance of the mountain called Giant. These involved on the spot interviews with locals, studio discussions with environmental experts, reports from pressure groups, as well as reviews of previous occurrences. The writing which emerged included newspaper reports, autocue resumés, geological diagrams, explanations, letters from locals, recounts in the parish chronicle and an article entitled 'Care for it or lose it' in the magazine 'England's Environment'. Choice is important in writing in role, since the imposition of a particular perspective does not sit comfortably with the variety of perspectives which will have been examined in the drama. These children selected the form, content, purpose and stance of their writing, in line with NC requirements, and exercised agency and autonomy in the process. The experience of the drama had given them something to say and the desire to communicate it, while their experience of literacy had given them knowledge of ways in which this might be written.

Drama in writing time

Through the use of drama conventions in the literacy hour and in extended writing time, ideas about the text can be spun into orbit and their reverberations examined. The ideas and possibilities voiced and improvised in this context will often be generated in pairs and small groups which offer security to young learners. As Heathcote (1995) has observed, drama operates in 'a no penalty zone', so children are free to improvise and imagine without fear of being judged and found wanting. Potentially, the compositional content of their later writing can be generated, shared and rehearsed in this time. A conversation for example, role-played into existence in the context of a fictional text, will begin to take a shape and form through the drama. If the teacher intervenes to build on this sensitively, then the eventual piece of collaboratively constructed writing will be much richer than individually produced writing without the generative and structural support of the drama. Much will depend however on the teacher's ability to create bridges between the drama and the writing.

A variety of bridging activities already exist, such as teacher modelling, joint composition, burst writing on white boards and the use of Post-it notes. Other types of bridges include the teacher summarising the knowledge gained about a character through the drama, or creating a writing frame to record the pros and cons of a situation generated first in a decision alley. Such bridging activities may capture the children's ideas as raw material and create a resource base for later use or may record them in a particular form which can then be imitated in their own writing. The teacher must also attend to the appropriacy of the chosen drama convention in relation to the selected form of writing, and the time and space given to the improvisational talk which generates, shares and rehearses the tune of the particular text. The process of travelling between drama and writing involves the following journey for young learners.

A plethora of drama conventions exist which can be harnessed to enrich and shape composition and effect in writing. These need to be flexibly handled in order to frame and shape meaning in the context of the text. They can be valuably employed in pairs or threes to help build engagement and insight, although each has different uses and operate to support context building, poetic, narrative and reflective modes of action in the drama (Neelands and Goode 2002). Particular conventions provoke and support particular kinds of writing: for example, thought tracking leads most easily into writing in the reflective mode, such as diary or letter writing in which a character's inner motivation and emotional perspective is revealed. Some conventions, however, have the potential to prompt several kinds of writing. Teachers therefore need to be conscious of the genre of the writing they are working towards and should employ drama conventions which will feed and develop that particular form. They also need to be conscious of the potential of the text and be able to dig down into its seams.

Mining the text's potential

Quality texts offer layers of meaning which drama can mine and forage. The work of Barrs and Cork (2001) has shown that three kinds of text make the richest contribution to writing: traditional folklore, emotionally powerful texts and texts comprised of poeticised speech. Such texts also offer rich resource material for classroom drama. Drama enables learners to explore the imaginary world of the text from the inside out, although the quality of the writing produced will in part depend upon the careful selection of a potentially rich and relevant moment in the text which resonates with the theme. A mundane moment will only develop limited imaginative engagement. A predicament of some potency must be in evidence since conflict and tension trigger the electricity of drama so, in choosing moments of ambiguity, challenge or misunderstanding, the teacher will enrich both the drama and the writing. Identifying gaps in the text can also help, for example unrecorded conversations, unmentioned thoughts, off the page scenarios, possible but undescribed meetings and so forth can be filled with meaning in the context of the text. Once a difficult moment has been selected, a particular drama convention can be employed to generate new insights, flesh out characters' thoughts and improvise possible scenarios.

Linking drama conventions to different forms of writing

1. **Role play** in pairs or small groups involves improvising an unrecorded conversation of some significance. This drama convention encourages children to use their knowledge of characters to compose orally or, if the text is new to them, to project certain characteristics onto the individuals, based on their life experience of similar situations or people.

The writing could include:

- a dialogue in the style of the text
- a play-script
- a persuasive letter
- reported speech.

For example, in *Clive and the Missing Finger* by Sarah Garland, Clive's dad reacts angrily to his daughter's painted face, 'she'd put on lipstick and there were peculiar orange patches down her cheekbones and black bits round her eyes'. He tells her to go upstairs and wash it off and unsurprisingly a row ensues. This can be partly read, improvised through role play and later recorded as a joint composition or through extended writing in pairs. The conversational context provides an opportunity to generate the row and to seek a conclusion to the altercation. Teaching about speech verbs, adverbs, the presentation of dialogue and the use of narrative action to enrich, frame and truncate conversation can be embedded in the class' composition.

"Go right upstairs and get that soppy mess off your face". Said dad angrily.

"Why should I, it looks gorgeous"! cried Dorrie.

"As gorgeous as a ducks bottom"! laughed Dad.

"Look, I don't care what you say I'm keeping it on"! wailed Dorrie.

"Why do you want that muck anyway? 'Dad asked

"Because all my friends hear it", groaned Dorrie

"But that necceserily doesn't make it right"

"But Dad I look silly if I'm the only girl whose not got it on"

"No you don't. I'll get you some proper makeup, 'Said Dad, understanding his daughter's predicament.

"Ok" agreed Dorrie reluctantly, "but you will let me choose, won't you?"

2. **Thought tracking** involves creating the inner thoughts of a character at a particular moment in a text. This can be organised with everyone taking on the persona of the character and voicing their thoughts simultaneously, or a chair can be placed in the centre of the class circle to represent that character. Children can then be invited to step forward and voice the role's thoughts aloud.

The writing could include:

- thought bubbles
- a prayer
- a diary entry
- a letter
- a monologue paragraph.

For example, in *Cliffhanger* by Jacqueline Wilson, poor Tim is lent upon my his macho sports-mad father to go on an adventure holiday. He is clearly not keen, but nonetheless his father books him a place. How does Tim feel the night before as he cuddles Walter Bear in bed and dreads the morning? In thinking through his worries, the class will be preparing to record these in his diary or in a letter to a friend about the dreaded holiday ahead.

3. **Freeze frames** involve creating still images or tableaux which show a narrative event as a flashback or flashforward. These may be dreams or desires, memories or anticipated events. Sequential freeze frames can depict the structure of the story or represent a historical time line of events, e.g. in the Second World War.

The writing could include:

- subtitles to create a text resumé
- a paragraph in the text
- a recount of the event depicted
- a newspaper article.

For example, in *Behind the Scenes at the Zoo* by Mark Craig and Christina MacDonald, freeze frames of possible photographs in the text can be made. Both the chapter title and the subtitle beneath the photographs can be generated and the paragraph which accompanies the text can be written by the group. This can then be compared with examples of the actual text.

4. **Storytelling in role** involves inventing and then retelling a story about another character from a particular role's perspective. It can prompt reflection upon the character's stance and allow children to build a possible narrative around an individual.

The writing could include:

- the story told
- reported speech in the context of the text
- a story map
- gossip in the context of the text.

For example, in *Rose meets Mr Wintergarten* by Bob Graham, when the Summers family move in next door to Mr Wintergarten they hear stories in the street about him. These can be planned and devised in twos and then with new partners the children can share their stories in role as locals, informing Mr and Mrs Summers about their neighbour. The class will need plenty of time to tell, retell, adapt and listen to each other's stories. Freeze frames of these could also be made.

5. **Decision alley** involves the class creating the thoughts or conscience of a character when faced with a momentous decision. Two lines of children face one another and voice the character's thoughts, both for and against the decision. One child, in role as the character, walks slowly up the alley and listens to their conscience before making the final decision.

The writing could include:

- a diary entry
- a letter of justification to another
- a paragraph which reflects the character's thinking
- a shape poem about the character.

For example, in *The Lion, The Witch and the Wardrobe* by C.S. Lewis, Edmund has to decide whether to go to the White Queen and betray his brother and sisters, or to remain with them and relinquish a possible kingdom and more Turkish Delight. His conflicting thoughts, desires and concerns can be voiced in the decision alley. This could be recorded as a diary entry or as a reflective passage in the text.

6. **Hot seating** a character involves all the class in adopting roles and asking questions of one character who is on the hot seat, in order to develop knowledge of their motives, attitudes and behaviour. The class need to take time to identify questions from their role perspective which will reveal more about the character. Several children can sit on the hot seat representing one character together.

The writing could include:

- a summary of the new knowledge generated
- a chapter/scenario using the facts and inferential insights
- a magazine interview
- a news article
- a poem to evoke the individual.

For example, in *The After Dark Princess* by Annie Dalton, Alice Fadzakerley, the perfect babysitter, is 'interviewed' by Mrs Quail who may want to employ her, but is concerned that her son Joe has never yet been left with a babysitter. The information gathered can be summarised around a silhouette of Alice, with facts and inferential insights listed separately (see below). A writing challenge could be to weave some of these characteristics and factual knowledge into a letter Mrs Quail writes to her sister, or into a later chapter in the text when Alice visits the Land of the After Dark.

Facts	*Inference/Opinion*
■ is 14 years old	is too good to be true
	is too perfect
■ is a girl guide	there's something mysterious about her
■ 2 brothers	appears sensible
■ First Aid certificate	is too able for a 14 year old
■ says she enjoys reading	when she lets her hair down she'll be wild
■ is very popular as a babysitter	cannot quite be sure of her
■ has a satchel and is tidy in appearance	there must be more to her or why would she
Year 5	be so popular?

7. **Role on the wall** involves building up information about a character over time as a novel is read or as a series of picture books with a recurring character are explored. A full size outline of one or more characters is drawn, using a child/adult lying on a large piece of paper. The space outside the outline can contain comments about the role from other characters' perspectives, the space inside the outline can capture the character's own attitudes and feelings at significant moments in the book/s. Role on the wall can create rich raw material for writing.

The writing could include:

■ verbatim quotes from the text

■ other characters' views

■ the role's thoughts and views

■ and could lead to letters, sociograms to reflect relationships or diary entries.

For example, if a number of wolf tales are being read, then the role on the wall could be Mr Wolf with various perspectives and insights shown from the various texts. These might include *The Last Wolf* by Michael Morpurgo, *Peter and the Wolf* retold by Ian Brett, *Little Wolf's Book of Badness* by Ian Whybrow, *Clever Polly and the Stupid Wolf* by Catherine Storr, and *The Three Little Wolves and the Big Bad Pig* by Eugene Trivias. The role in the wall will create an effective summary across these texts and will provide ideas, phrases and perspectives about the character of the wolf in these stories.

8. **Group improvisation** involves the spontaneous or prepared generation of ideas and action. It may involve creating a future scenario in the narrative or could be in the form of a flashback. Chapter titles suit group improvisations, as they often act as hints or precursors in the text and usefully prefigure later scenarios, but what happens next is also possible to improvise.

The writing could include:

- a plan for the chapter
- a paragraph or two
- a flashback into the past
- a play-script of the scene.

For example, in *Ruby the Rudest Girl in the World*, *Boris the Brainiest Boy* or *Cinderboy*, all by Laurence Anholt, the next significant narrative action in the text could be predicted at various points. What happens, for example, when Cinderboy's magical TV godmother intervenes in his exclusion from the Big Cup Final? A group improvisation of future narrative action in the text can lead to the shaping of events and possible paragraphs or a play-script to capture these events.

9. **Formal meetings** involve whole class improvisations in the context of an imagined context. Such meetings can include press conferences, council meetings, court scenes, public events, an animal council, a staff meeting and so on. Formal meetings need the teacher in role to set the context, to challenge thinking and to make the situation more complex.

The writing could include:

- notes or minutes from the meeting
- official records
- a newspaper report
- press releases or posters
- letters protesting against or supporting the motion.

For example, in *Holes* by Louis Sachar, a mystery surrounds the warden and the forced labour which the inmates of Camp Green Lake Juvenile Correction Facility are obliged to undertake. By adding the idea that a group of journalists might have heard rumours about the conditions there and might arrive unannounced to interview the management, a fictional context is given for a press conference. News reports, camp records, notes and letters of complaint could all be written following the meeting. The following are two examples of children's writing.

Omar Dhillon
8T

Mr Sir's diary extract
after the conference

After this absolutly pointless session with the paparazzi not much had been achieved by them. There were also questions put towards I and the coarden of which not many were a tough challenge to answer. Some of these irrelevant questions included things about why myself and the coarden work these prisoners and how we would like it if our children came to this camp etc... etc...

When I next saw the coarden I asked him what he thought of the conference. His reply was plain, and un emotional. 'Rubbish - pointless - pathetic'

I rethought carefully about the questions asked at the conference. Suddenly, a supposed innocent prisoner Stanley came into mind, could the paparazzi talk the coarden and I out of running camp Green Lake and finding out buried treasure in the dried lake.

The coarden and I must talk this over — there is something mysterious happening?

Jamie
Pethick 8T

Mr Sir's diary

17TH July 2000

What a load of lies that press conference was. Burgers for lunch, ha, medical care, what a load of rubbish. They eat stale bread and we don't even know basic first aid.

If they really knew what was going on, if they really knew we were getting those little criminals to dig holes to find us treasure, they would never stop bothering us about it.

They don't find much in big hauls anyway. Even if they do find something we tell them we give it to an antiques shop, or to a charity. Fools!

That Stanley boy is drawing a lot of attention to himself, but we'll soon stop that. A little less water will soon shut him up.

10. **Group sculpture** involves children in creating an image which reflects a key theme in the text. Collectively, they share their views and construct a shape which conveys the often abstract or moral issues underpinning the tale. Such shapes can be 'made' of particular materials which help to convey further layers of meaning, e.g. wire, cloth, wood, stone, marble, cotton wool, clay, concrete.

The writing could include:

■ titles and commentaries

■ an explanatory plaque

■ a descriptive paragraph

■ a letter explaining the sculpture.

For example, in the picture books *Falling Angels* by Colin Thompson and *The Boy and the Cloth of Dreams* by Jenny Koralek, a number of themes will emerge. These can be discussed and created in group sculptures and subtitled or summarised afterwards.

Sculpture titles from *The Boy and the Cloth of Dreams*

■ growing up

■ childhood dying

■ the death of fear

■ a loving family helps you

■ afraid today, confident tomorrow (Year 6).

Drama and writing

As a multimodal art form, drama uses visual and verbal literacy and the languages of movement and sound to make meaning. These dramatic literacies help children develop their imaginative capacity both in speech and writing. Through making their thinking visible in drama, children are more confidently able to voice their views and in-role perspectives and make connections to the real world from dwelling thoughtfully inside a fictional one (Grainger and Kendall-Seatter 2003). Drama can make a real contribution to the process of composition and offers opportunities to generate and share ideas as well as rehearse them orally in the chosen genre. Through this process children experience the shape of their own argument or perspective and focus on fluency and the extension and clarification of meaning. As writers they begin to discover what they want to say.

In order to enrich children's engagement in writing and to enliven their prose, teachers can make fuller use of the affective power of drama to shape and construct meaning. It must be recognised however, that drama is much more than a pre-writing activity: it is a symbolic art form which seeks to investigate, question and reflect upon meaning. If drama, the art form of social encounters, is used merely as a method of enriching writing, its scope and power will be reduced. Drama offers young writers significant compositional support; it should be employed both widely and wisely.

References

Barrs, M. and Cork, V. (2001) *The Reader in the Writer*. London: CLPE.

Craft, A., Jeffrey, B. and Liebling, M. (2001) *Creativity in Education*. London: Continuum.

DfEE (1999) *The National Curriculum for England and Wales*. London: DfEE.

Grainger, T. (2001) 'Drama and Writing I: Imagination on the Page', *The Primary English Magazine*, April, 6–10.

Grainger, T. (2003) 'Exploring the unknown, ambiguity, interaction and meaning making in classroom drama' in Bearne, E., Dombey, H. and Grainger, T. *Classroom Interactions in Literacy*. Buckingham: OUP.

Grainger, T. and Cremin, M. (2001) *Resourcing Classroom Drama 5–8*. Sheffield: NATE.

Grainger, T. and Kendall-Seatter, S. (2003) 'Drama and Spirituality: Some reflective connections', *The International Journal of Spirituality*, 8.

Heathcote, D. and Bolton, G. (1995) *Drama for learning*. Portsmouth: Heinemann.

McNaughton, M. J. (1997) 'Drama and Writing: A study of the influence of drama on the imaginative writing of primary school children', *Research in Drama Education*, 2, 55–86.

Neelands, J. and Goode, T. (2002) *Structuring Drama Work*, 2nd edn. Cambridge: Cambridge University Press.

O'Neill, C. (1995) *Drama Worlds*. London: Heinemann.

Chapter 11

Dance and the literacy curriculum

Jill Newbald with Prue Goodwin

In Physical Education (PE) children are encouraged to be as successful as possible in all aspects of movement. The English National Curriculum (DfEE 1999) requires different aspects of PE to be included at different ages and caters for different levels of ability. Dance is one of these requirements within the programme of study for PE. At primary level, children are required to 'respond to a range of stimuli and accompaniment' and 'suggest improvements based on what makes a performance effective'. As one of the three key elements of PE in the primary school, dance makes a unique contribution to children's learning. It is the one aspect of the PE curriculum which relates to expression of feelings, thoughts and ideas through the way in which the body can move. The language used to describe the movement and the visual and dramatic way in which the body is used independently or within a group, are all exclusive to the individual performing the dance. Such expressive activities can provide a rich context for the development of language. Children can discuss and explore ideas about effectively using the body's movements to translate their understanding. The concepts that they translate into movement may be extremely complex, possibly beyond their capacity to express in spoken or written forms. From the initial stages of the dance to the final performance, children are constantly using language to refine and extend their movement sequences. By its very nature, dance requires children to be active participants – developing, reviewing and performing their ideas. The physical nature of this process places such activities firmly within PE but, because it is a form of expression which engages children in a creative experience, it also facilitates the development of language through children's exploration, for example, of space, shape, form, time and rhythm.

Meaning in movement

As movement is a child's first form of expression, with the body being the only means to achieve this, young children are encouraged to explore the full range of movement that their bodies can make. This occurs quite spontaneously and children generally become aware of space, body shapes, and recognise which parts of their bodies can help to perform certain movements. As they begin to control and refine these movements, children use them to express and communicate different feelings, moods and ideas. 'Dance has a language of its own, one without words – body talk!' (Harrison 1993: 14).

In order to develop their dance potential, children need to be given opportunities to experience movement in contexts that take them beyond their own natural activity through play. As children begin to understand the world around them, they gain awareness of movement characteristics, for example, how a cat stalks its prey or how a mouse scurries away with its cheese. They will also observe movements which are commonly used as a means of human expression, for example, how we clutch hold of someone in a moment of fear or how our bodies slump in depression. Our use of words frequently adds to the 'feel' of movements. 'Tip toe' or 'clitter-clatter' clearly indicate what sort of movement they portray. This growing store of gestures, movements and words may later provide a means of expressing particular feelings or ideas through organised movement – dance.

Providing children with a stimulating environment within which they can experience such movement opportunities and making them aware of how these can affect their senses will provide rich experiences and backgrounds to which they can refer. It is not only words and sounds that reflect the movements they describe but other art forms all contribute towards children's growing awareness of shape, sound, texture and rhythm – the key elements of dance. Many of the words and expressions used in music, art, sculpture and literacy are borrowed for use in dance, and the links between the creative arts are clear to see.

Dance in the literacy curriculum

Within the primary curriculum, dance is not about training dancers; it is about educating through movement, whether it be used as a starting point which may then stimulate work or as a means to furthering understanding of themes being studied across the curriculum. It could be argued that, of all school subjects, PE and English are the most similar in that they develop continuously from conception and that they benefit greatly from, but are not dependent on, outside intervention (i.e. education) in order to develop. The essential linguistic and physical skills are acquired through purposeful activity which, in the formal setting of school, may also be associated with learning in any other subjects. Children involved in dance, whilst working on movement skills, are provided with a vehicle for many aspects of the English curriculum, particularly speaking and listening:

- discussion, collaboration, negotiation

- listening and responding to others' ideas
- working as a member of a group
- evaluating and selecting ideas
- extending ideas in the light of discussion
- being reflective and critical in order to improve
- recognising and celebrating success.

Reading and writing are equally supported. Dance offers a means of responding to reading and can work as a source of inspiration for writing. It provides opportunities for children to develop their understanding of a theme or concept by offering a basis upon which language and ideas can originate. Movement and dance can also be incorporated into the presentation of research. The English work and dance are mutually beneficial. It is not only the product or performance that is important in dance; everything that goes into the development of the dance in order to make the performance as effective as possible, especially the discussions, are rich learning opportunities for both PE and English.

Dancing the text

A dance idea can originate from almost any text being studied or created. In particular, children's responses to stories and poems can be greatly enhanced by dance. It can be used to communicate their feelings or moods about what they have read or heard as well as to develop their understanding. However, children need a foundation from which to develop their work. Just as a child could not paint a mountain landscape without first knowing something about mountains, or write a poem about snow if they had never seen or felt snow, nor could they create a dance about something of which they have no previous experience. When setting out to respond or create through dance, teachers should aim to use other art forms and engage all the senses to assist children's understanding and guide their responses. As with literacy, the adult should model and share experiences alongside the learners before expecting independent work to take place.

A child cannot 'be' a river or a tree. Yet, they can perform actions such as waving or swirling which represent the movement of the water or branches. Their experience of running water or branches being blown by the wind provides them with the knowledge of how to imitate these movements. Equally children cannot 'be' machines (a theme which is often used as part of work on the Industrial Revolution which might include stories of working children in factories), but they can experiment with the repetitive, organised actions typical of mechanical operations. Words, sounds and pictures would be useful stimuli. Concepts which are abstract may also become clearer to children through the combination of sights, sounds and movement. For example, using an extract from Thomas Hood's poem, 'The Song of the Shirt' (in Jerrold 1911), can provide an initial stimulus to a dance sequence about the repetitive motions of machines and the repetitive day-to-day lives of the working class people during the Industrial Revolution.

> With fingers weary and worn,
> With eyelids heavy and red,
> A woman sat, in unwomanly rags,
> Plying her needle and thread-
> Stitch! stitch! stitch!
> In poverty, hunger, and dirt,
> And still with the voice of delorous pitch
> She sang the 'Song of the Shirt!'

The language and pattern of the poem, together with its theme, clearly describe the repetition in the woman's life and the conditions of working class people at that time. It could inspire the children's responses with strong, short, easy to repeat, and direct movements. Short movement motifs can then be invented, selected and repeated. These can be developed showing further consideration for size, speed, level and shape of movements, together with relationships to other characters and to any accompaniment.

There are many examples of how dance can help children engage with texts. Indeed, sometimes a text 'cries out' to be interpreted through movement. For example:

- The short story *The Great Piratical Rumbustification* (Mahy 1981) which concerns a party for pirates. Throughout the tale there are characters and scenes that can be interpreted through movement, especially the lines: 'They turned the footpaths of the city into a pirate chain-dance, they turned the streets into a pirate parade. Suddenly the city seemed to twist and spin and sing like a big humming top.' The patterns of a chain dance can be quite formal, providing a 'framework' for younger, less experienced pupils whilst there is also an opportunity to explore moving to the sailors' hornpipe and sea shanties.

- In the first chapter of *The Firework-Maker's Daughter* (Pullman 1996) we hear how Lila wanted to make fireworks. The fireworks have wonderfully evocative names: Crackle-Dragons, Leaping Monkeys, Golden Sneezes, Tumble Demons, Shimmering Coins. As an introduction to this exciting tale, children can interpret the names through movement, art and music.

- Pupils researching the effect of deforestation on the environment could demonstrate the plight of farmers who had lost land by creating a dance sequence.

- Children can tackle the complex language of the witches' scenes in *Macbeth* whilst planning their 'dance' around the cauldron.

The following description of lessons based on *The Iron Man* illustrates just one book that inspired response through dance.

The Iron Man by Ted Hughes

As part of their literacy work, a class of eight- and nine-year-old children were examining different settings for stories. They had listened to the first chapter of *The Iron Man* by Ted Hughes and had discussed the unusual setting of this story and the author's use of language to create the atmosphere. Based on Hughes' description and their own imaginations, the children were asked to make charcoal sketches of their impression of the Iron Man. These pictures were later developed using chalk and three-dimensional models were created on a large scale.

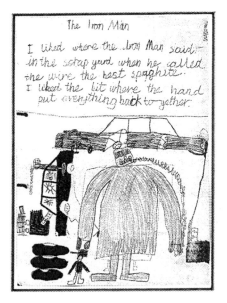

'The Iron Man came to the top of the cliff'

In the following dance session, the children began by exploring different sorts of travelling movements – small, light, quick, darting, using zigzag pathways, large, heavy, slow, powerful, controlled, angular, robotic. These movements led naturally into contrasting body shapes. Having decided which movements were most suited to the Iron Man, each child created a short movement phrase – going forwards, then backwards – which could easily be repeated and developed into a swaying movement or one of stillness. Each child was beginning to appreciate how difficult it was for the Iron Man to move because of his size and the immobility of a body made of iron.

'Down the cliff the Iron Man came toppling, head over heels'

The children were reminded about the Iron Man falling off the cliff and the ricochet of metal before it landed, a twisted, heap of iron debris. In order to be able to control their fall (as if from the cliff), children explored different speeds of movements, starting with light, quick, flicking of fingers only, then hands, arms, legs and finally short, sharp movements of whole body. They then tried to produce heavy movements in slow motion using the whole hand, leg or body with a twisting rather than bending of joints. This was developed into a sequence following from the swaying movement as the Iron Man lost his balance and fell from the cliff. The children decided where to include the moment of ricochet within their sequence – a sudden, sharp reaction before continuing to a low level where the body lay twisted and still.

At this point, the children worked as response partners, evaluating the performance of a friend with comments about the effectiveness of the movements chosen and how they might be improved. This sharing of work provided an opportunity for them to learn from each other's ideas. Having reached this stage, the dance could have been considered complete based on the individual work that had been done. However, the opportunity to work in pairs and groups would extend discussion of the text and would be a very effective way of putting the Iron Man figure back together again.

'Slowly the hand crept over the stones, searching'

The children were split into groups which would 'become' two arms, two legs, two hands and eyes around an imagined 'body' so that the Iron Man would become a whole figure once again. The shape was produced horizontally, lying on the floor.

The final reassembly of the figure meant the whole dance could be performed. In terms of the PE curriculum, the children had devised and developed several movement sequences, which they had gradually refined. They had co-operated with other members of their group and worked as a class on the final performance. The concentration and physical control involved in listening to the music and getting the timing right took considerable effort for some children. However, no matter what they had achieved related to PE, every child had a clearer understanding, and a deeper appreciation, of the wonderful language in the opening chapter of *The Iron Man*.

Conclusion

There are many advantages to incorporating dance into the literacy curriculum. For example, dance:

- offers a means of enabling children to respond imaginatively to texts they have read;
- helps children generate ideas and vocabulary for writing;
- particularly supports the children who are powerful kinaesthetic learners by encouraging them to use their bodies in conjunction with their developing linguistic skills;
- broadens the learning experience for all children, offering a different dimension from which to view written language;
- provides a purposeful context for revisiting and discussing text (an essential way of developing the ability to read beyond the literal).

Above all, the liberation and joy of dance provides the context for many children to experience the pleasures to be had from creative engagement with good literature.

Acknowledgement

We are grateful to the pupils of Bushy High Junior School, Guildford, for their work on *The Iron Man*.

References

DfEE (1999) *The National Curriculum: handbook for primary teachers*. London: DfEE.

Harrison, K. (1993) *Let's Dance*. Sevenoaks: Hodder & Stoughton.

Hughes, T. (1987) *The Iron Man*. London: Faber & Faber.

Jerrold, W. (ed.) (1911) *The Complete Poetical Works of Thomas Hood*. Oxford: Oxford University Press.

Mahy, M. (1981) *The Great Piratical Rumbustification and The Librarian and the Robbers*. London: Puffin.

Pullman, P. (1996) *The Firework-Maker's Daughter*. London: Transworld Publishing.

Chapter 12

The potential and possibilities of musical and physical literacies

Angela Pickard and Justine Earl

This chapter argues for connections between body and mind and the need to return to the exploration of a wide vision of literacy and what it is to be literate. It is time to examine the effect of a prescriptive curriculum that is heavily focused on raising standards in reading, writing and maths. Although the desire to raise standards in key areas is commendable, it is necessary to question if such a narrow view of what it is to be literate is really offering our children a truly broad and balanced curriculum. A wider vision of literacy, one that places creativity, imagination and innovative thinking at the heart of every teaching and learning experience, will once again empower teachers and children to consider exciting new possibilities.

We are arguing that the languages of music and dance are rich and powerful in their own right. However, there are obvious links between literacy (speaking and listening as well as reading and writing), music and dance. By holding fast to a broad view of what constitutes a 'text' so that it includes the reading and creating of music and dance compositions, teachers are able to lead children towards literacy events which go beyond rigid prescription. There are similarities between the creation of word, music or movement based texts. All require the author, composer or choreographer to make decisions relating to many aspects, for example structure, audience, purpose and style. The process of composition starts with an initial idea or stimulus. What we create is influenced greatly by what we have read, seen, heard or felt. The need to make emotional connections, to explain events and experiences is part of what it is to be human. Stories help us to do this. In this chapter we wish to explore the language of music and dance and the connections between conventional narratives and music and dance compositions. By drawing on shared narrative experiences, children can reach deeper and more satisfying levels of response and understanding.

The language of music

Music is important. It makes little difference if it is the Latin rhythms of the Salsa or Samba, the intense, relentlessness of house or techno or the sweeping grandeur of a classical symphony. Music is important. It is a powerful language with which children want to connect and it must fill the classroom as often as possible. When children experience music, it is exactly that: an experience. They will want to move, to talk, to explore, to mimic, to extend. It matters little what style of music is chosen, response is inevitable and it will be rich in emotions. After experiencing a piece of music with others (particularly, we could argue, one which does not involve the use of words) there will be much discussion. Ideas will be shared, perhaps beginning with 'It makes me feel...' or 'It makes me think of...'.

In the same way that children are asked to read literature, a piece of music is a text that can be 'read'. The shared reading of a piece of music will allow children to explore their perceptions of and responses to a musical composition. True, the elements of music may not be the same as the features of fiction but there is no reason why the language of one 'text' cannot be used to enrich an understanding of another. Whilst not suggesting that music is only valuable in the primary classroom if it can be used to enhance our teaching of literacy, it is possible to see how linking musical with written compositions may enrich the understanding of and response to both text types. For example, children who are able to select and justify their choice of a musical theme suitable for a well-known character from a book are demonstrating a deep understanding of both the character and the music. The ensuing discussion of the choice, supported by appropriate metalanguage, will only serve to develop this understanding further as well as to allow use of language to reflect, analyse and interpret.

When engaged in listening and responding to music, children's discussions will often involve exploring the elements of

- structure
- pitch
- rhythm
- dynamics
- tempo
- timbre
- texture.

As they compose, their creative endeavour will include making choices related to all these aspects; considering how they wish their piece to be structured, selecting instruments to use to provide the required sound quality, deciding the volume of sound at certain points as well as the overall style and speed. As the process of composition unfolds, children engage in evaluation and they will refine their work. After performing to others, they make changes. This requires a common vocabulary with which to describe the effectiveness of the composition and the proficiency of the performance. This shared language is also needed when listening to pieces of music, whether recorded or live. In the same way, literacy sessions encourage the development of the language of analysis and evaluation. Children are asked to comment on the effectiveness of writing they encounter.

Music has long been connected with stories – whether it is used to set a scene, to evoke a place or time, to communicate feelings, to denote action or to describe a particular character. The term programme music dates from the time of Liszt, although music connected with literary ideas existed much earlier than the mid-nineteenth century. This includes sixteenth century descriptive choral pieces such as Jannequin's *The Hare Hunt* and *The Song of the Birds* as well as Haydn's introduction to the oratorio *The Creation* entitled 'Chaos'. A well known example of programme music is Beethoven's 'Pastoral' Symphony, with a first movement entitled 'Awakening of happy feelings on arrival in the country'. This symphony clearly suggests aspects of the countryside – although Beethoven himself described the piece as 'the expression of feelings rather than painting'. Since Liszt, many composers have offered us pieces that connect with features of narrative, such as Mendelssohn's *Midsummer Night's Dream* overture, Saint-Saens' *Danse Macabre*, Rimsky-Korsakof's *Sheherazarde* and much work by Berlioz, Strauss and Copland.

Of course, some classical pieces such as ballet or film music are composed specifically to support the telling of a tale and as such are rich resources for connecting with literacy.

Making connections

Some compositions provide easy starting points for linking music and the features of narrative. For example, a shared reading of the music written by Howard Blake to accompany the animated version of Raymond Briggs' *The Snowman* allows exploration of the choices the composer made. The overall structure of the composition can be related to the structure of the animated and the picture book texts. Children can discuss how the music matches the changing action of the story as well as how the emotions communicated by both versions are affected by the addition of music. What is the effect of particular themes? Can the children identify when these themes return? What sort of setting is being described by the music and how can the listener tell? Which sections of the music are clearly describing actions and which are more evocative of emotions? Blake's music is so much more than the addition of sound effects. When children are asked to create sound effects for a particular story under the guise of linking music and language, such an activity is not sufficiently creative and often becomes a far too literal experience. Children who undertake group compositions stimulated by a story will be developing their expressive as well as their functional language as they explore, compare, negotiate, describe, reflect and evaluate.

Many other classical pieces of music support the telling of a whole tale such as Dukas' *The Sorcerer's Apprentice* and Prokofief's *Peter and the Wolf*.

Structure

Children can represent the structure of a piece of music by drawing; just as they might story map a written or oral tale. Comparisons can be made between sections of a story and sections of a music composition. Different types of endings or beginnings can be experienced and their effect discussed. As young writers and composers try to express in words the type of ending they have heard, they may well be able to draw parallels with endings of stories they have read. Does the musical ending sound very final because of the use of repeated strong chords and/or a perfect cadence? What stories do they know that end in this way, with no room for uncertainty? Or does the piece have a surprising ending, like a cliffhanger at the end of a story? Perhaps the music fades away, without a resounding ending at full volume. What sort of story might end like this and why? Children can be involved in composing music to match part of a story, but equally they may write or identify a story that mirrors part or all of a piece of music.

Character

Composers sometimes evoke a character by linking them to a particular theme. This musical use of an *idée fixe* or leitmotiv can be explored with children. For example, the character of Rosie the hen in Pat Hutchins' classic text *Rosie's Walk* appears to remain constant throughout the text despite the antics of the fox. Indeed, the pictorial representation changes very little. The composition of 'Rosie's Theme' would not only allow a creative, musical experience for the children, but would necessitate a detailed exploration of her character. What do they think she is really aware of as she goes for her walk? What might be going through her mind? What is Rosie really like: a passive, unsuspecting actor in this pantomime or is she totally in control of the situation? Of course, children can be and are challenged to read between the lines when they explore quality picture books in literacy sessions without linking to music. However, by taking the next step and adding another dimension – another language – the literacy experience is enriched and taken to new depths. Such composition or selection of a musical theme also supports those who prefer to express their thoughts and ideas in ways without words.

In a similar way, music written to link with a particular character in a play, ballet or film can be useful starting points in literacy. By listening to the Princess Leia theme written by John Williams for the first *Star Wars* film, children can discuss what sort of character is being evoked. It is then possible to examine the use of music in film as they listen out for snatches of the theme within the actual film. This recognises the importance of multiple literacies and the wide-ranging resources available to the teacher of literacy. Teaching of language must go beyond prescription, routine and inflexible approaches if it is to engage and motivate the children and the teacher.

Setting

If children can select or compose a piece of music which they feel best represents a setting, then they are demonstrating an ability to visualise, experience and articulate their perception of a place they have only met through a written text. Of course, they may have experienced the setting through drama activities before they come to express it musically. Again, we will want to encourage them to go beyond the literal as they compose and the effectiveness of their pieces will rely much on a good understanding of the written text as well as the possibilities that music offers. They may well move from the concrete towards the abstract. Such exciting developments in thought and musical ideas will surely enrich the experiences of both art forms.

The language of dance

If we agree that learning is a creative activity, a process of exploration, discovery, problem solving and representation of knowledge, experience and thinking in a variety of ways, then opportunities for movement and dance are essential to learning.

Babies explore with movement, space and their senses to make connections with their environment. They are natural movers and experiment creatively by extending fingers and hands, kicking at different speeds, reaching out, gesturing and adding sounds to communicate. Infants and toddlers are determined and self-motivated to communicate what they know and can do with their whole body (Post and Hohmann 2000).

Young children learn through doing and talking, experimenting and representing their shared knowledge and individual experiences through using dance and rhythm (Slade 1954). Beyond imitation and copying, children play with ideas and engage in creative and imaginative processes, developing a greater understanding that movement is language as they deepen their sense of self in the physical world.

On a daily basis, children will encounter and engage with opportunities to develop greater co-ordination and control over their movements and manipulation of objects, at home and at school. As children increase their understanding of their body in action, they will engage in greater exploration of actions, feelings, body shapes, gestures, space and respond to a variety of sounds, rhythms and beats thereby sequencing phrases of movement. Improving the quality of movements can be encouraged through a process of planning, composing, performing and reviewing.

Anyone can make up a dance, all they need is an idea, but sometimes this is the most difficult thing to decide upon. An obvious source of ideas are stories. By drawing on previous real life and textual experiences, children can lift known images, feelings, words, rhythms and structures, re-call and connect with them, wiggle them in their fingers, squiggle them in their toes, meander in and out of the texts and make old and new stories come to life. Through their physical, creative and imaginative responses, they can create new patterns of meaning and representation (Policastro and Gardner 1999). Here, children are reading between the lines of the texts of their lives and pushing the boundaries of meaning, as the boundaries in dance, like those in play, are broad and fluid.

Making dances involves planning, interpreting, improvising, rehearsing and expressing. Choices are made in an energetic choreographic process of selection and rejection in order to try new ways of telling a story, express feelings or moods or say something through the visual representation of movement. A combination of leaning on and building upon both shared and individual experience engages the maker and spectator in sharing meaning making. Decisions in relation to:

- body parts
- directions
- floor patterns
- levels of movement
- timing, rhythm or sound
- relationships
- dynamics

may need to be made. For example, it is difficult to convey sadness through fast, balanced and light movements; more appropriate would be movements giving into gravity with contrasted tense and relaxed movements at a slow speed.

It is essential that children have opportunities and challenges in order to search, select, shape, share and shift through movement. In doing so, they are developing an exciting and enriching vocabulary in relation to:

- body parts
- basic body actions – balance, gesture, jump, roll, turn, travel
- action – verbs: spiral, meander, stomp
- space – on spot, travelling, floor patterns and shapes, levels
- time
- quality of movement – adverbs: quickly, powerfully, lightly
- response and evaluation.

The dynamics of dance can be thought of rather like the colours of a painting: they create points of interest and contrast as well as expressing much of the meaning. For example, varying the speed in a dance or contrasting the use of off-balance movements that portray a sense of urgency and vitality, with balanced positions that allow the audience a moment of rest. Rhythm or pattern is important in dance as it often has its own rhythm within its composition through repeated phrases of movement, linked to speed. We need to see some pattern in things in order to understand them, so a lack of rhythm is associated with chaos or disjointedness. We sense rhythm in the beating of a heart, breathing patterns, waves on the shore and more formally, in poetry, storytelling, children's literature and music.

Part of making dances is to present and communicate them to others, as part of the whole class or in smaller groups, after all dance is a performing art. Here the focus should be on an enjoyment of sharing rather than a disciplined, rehearsed performance and, just as in response to writing time, children's evaluative comments should be constructive and sensitive.

Connecting, communicating and composing

The themes, plot development, characters and settings of many fairy tales can be used as areas of musical, physical, creative and imaginative exploration, development and composition. The use of role play areas, drama techniques and process drama are all instrumental tools in the development of children's physical responses. However, to create and communicate through the language of dance, movement vocabulary, dynamics and choreographic devices can be utilised. Exploring body shape, space and speed, considering the quality of a movement in relation to its weight or flow and incorporating devices such as unison, canon and repetition, are all ways of interacting and engaging with the process that is choreography.

Fairy tales

The following suggested ideas for using fairy tales as a stimulus for creative music and dance can be adapted, selected and rejected to suit individual needs and experience. We have taken the story of Cinderella and the books *Little Red Riding Wolf* by Laurence Anholt and Arthur Robbins, and *Snow White in New York* by Fiona French to provide examples.

Cinderella

Music

Great composers such as Mozart, Schumann, Puccini, Rossini, Tchaikovsky, Wagner, Humperdink and Offenbach have taken fairy tales as their subject matter. Music is a key element in Disney's popular animated film versions. The seven elements of music could be investigated in relation to this familiar fairy tale, depending on the age and stage of the children, in order to represent character traits, structure and plot.

Dance

This well known fairy tale can be used to engage children in creating characters and narrative through movement and gesture simply by drawing on key events to structure and focus the physical representation.

Plot

Cleaning – A series of appropriate work related actions could be explored and developed into a sequence, such as, rhythmic sweeping backwards and forwards, slow, staggering steps while carrying a heavy basket of washing, chopping wood, and vigorous scrubbing and polishing.

Dressing for the ball – In role as an ugly sister, children could engage in miming a series of searching for particular items of clothing for the ball, trying them on, looking in the mirror, changing their mind and finally settling on dresses and accessories for the ball. Freeze frames could be posed and then a sequence composed with linking movements.

Transformation – From a low, curled position, children could gradually grow and stretch high and wide, turning slowly on the spot – Cinderella now has a beautiful gown. Tiptoeing, scuttling and running mice, travelling in and around the space, sudden freezes as they are touched by magic. Light, rhythmic, trotting horses could emerge and move individually, making their own shapes and floor pattern in the space.

The palace and ballroom – Familiar step patterns and sequences from folk or country dances or a waltz could be used to engage in the ballroom dancing scene moving into a duet between Cinderella and Prince Charming. Here children could explore walking slowly towards a partner, pausing, making eye contact and reaching towards them, gently lifting their partner's hands and lowering them. This could be developed by pairs taking it in turn to lead and follow and change directions, with and without holds. Children could stand opposite each other and copy or mirror each other's actions such as, walking towards, walking away from each other, walking forward, back and stepping side to side. Turning could also be added.

Midnight strikes – The use of a repetitive rhythm, regular paused movements, like the ticking of a clock, with arms, legs or the whole body, in a circular, clockwise motion, could be developed. Moving forwards, backwards and from side to side like a metronome could also be suggested. Twelve strong, vertical pulls with arms or whole body swings could indicate midnight.

Happy ever after – Plodding with big, flat, floppy feet, tiptoeing, hopping, overbalancing and falling over as the glass slipper is tried and found to be either too big or too small. Then, the children could walk elegantly as the shoe fits. The duet between Cinderella and Prince Charming could also be repeated here. A deeper engagement and interpretation of the emotions of the character of Cinderella or the conflict and tension that exists between Cinderella and her ugly sisters could also be considered further.

Emotions of Cinderella – Loneliness, sadness and tiredness could be examined and explored through slow, careful, controlled, smooth travelling and turning movements. Slow walking and turning, stopping, sighing, droopy, slumped shapes and finally drops to the floor through exhaustion, could become the basis for the sequence.

Tension with sisters – Investigating transference of weight leading to dropping to the floor, rolling and onto feet again is the beginning of a trio based on weight bearing and push and pull. The children could play with balance and counter balance initially with a partner, then as a three through trust exercises where each other can easily support weight. Loss of balance, rolling, leaning onto each other, supporting, pushing and pulling could be investigated and a sequence where Cinderella is pushed and pulled between the ugly sisters could be created.

Little Red Riding Wolf

Music – An exploration of pitch, duration, dynamics and tempo in relation to the characters and theme could set the context for compositions. By communicating moods and qualities of the characters, children could accompany the dance pieces.

Dance – This parody text can be used as a stimulus for communicating different moods and feelings through the use of different body shapes and gestures in relation to characters and theme.

Little Wolfie's character – Actions such as prancing, low jumping, high and low skipping, galloping and side stepping, with a light, bouncy quality could be explored and developed to convey the cute, sweet and happy nature of the wolf cub. Meandering along a path, stopping to smell flowers, smiling and waving could be added.

Big Bad Girl's character – Actions such as slow, heavy stomping, plodding, waiting gestures, shrugging shoulders, deep sighing and hunched sitting could be investigated to convey the weighted, cross, and bored nature of the girl.

Theme of strong and weak – Striding, confident, tough, firm and forceful movements and dynamics could be explored and developed. A strong, powerful travelling sequence with definite rhythm, sharp turns, clear direction with head up could be created. In contrast, delicate, feeble, fragile, soft and timid movements could be explored and developed. A frightened, cautious, tiptoeing travelling sequence with erratic rhythm, tenuous turns, with no clear direction and head down could be created.

Theme of bullying – Working in pairs, freeze frames of actions when Little Wolfie meets the Big Bad Girl could be developed. A sequence of three freeze frames could be choreographed. A consideration of linking movements and flow between the frames, the tension that exists between the characters and attention to strong and weak qualities and gestures could be evaluated. The piece could be developed further by examining action and reaction by moving around, over and under each other.

Snow White in New York by Fiona French

Music – Fiona French uses the contrast of dark and light to great effect in this text. It not only indicates good and evil, in terms of character, but spotlights key moments of the plot. Children can be challenged to compose or select music that evokes either the dark and the malevolent or the light and the positive.

Dance – This version of Snow White set in 1920s New York could be used to consider setting further and has potential for an exploration of different dance styles. An opportunity to connect to and communicate different moods and feelings through an examination of the stepmother's anger and jealousy is also possible.

New York skyline – Working in twos or threes with body contact, lines, shapes, angles, directions and the contours of different skylines and architecture, as illustrated in the text, could be examined. The use of symmetry and asymmetry to encourage a variety of outlines could be considered. Working in larger groups, a sequence of interesting skylines, moving from one to another with different transitions could be created. Changes in rhythm and speed, weight, flow and use of space could be developed and evaluated.

Different dance styles – The Charlston, Lindy Hop and jazz style could form the basis for an investigation into steps, patterns, mood, formation, design and choreography. The use of a video resource, such as the film and musical *Bugsy Malone*, or, if possible, a demonstration from a dance development worker or indeed a professional company, in order to view and examine some steps would be helpful. Children could be involved in the identification, copying and repeating of movements, steps and sequences then using this material to develop their own versions. High, explosive jumps, different ways of holding, supporting, leaning, pushing, pulling and lifting a partner, teamed with fast footwork and a high energy, both in music choices and choreography could make exciting viewing, participation and evaluation.

Anger and jealousy – Tension in the body should be maintained while executing stamping, kicking, jumping, rocking, banging, slapping the ground, clenched fists and punching movements. Facial expressions could be developed and the children could engage in pulling faces, frowning and grimacing. Words to accentuate movements and feelings such as 'I feel f . . . u . . . r . . . i . . . o . . . u . . . s!' could be added. Choreographing a piece that communicates the emotions of the character could contain the previously explored travelling movements, freezes in strong, twisty, spiky and angular shapes, slow turns, gestures and explosive jumps. Attention to facial expressions and the rhythms, weight and tension would develop the qualities and dynamics of the piece.

Fairy Tale Wood

Music – A fairy tale wood is a fascinating setting. It is a place of transformations, as explored by Sondheim in his 1987 musical *Into the Woods*. It is a place of fear and uncertainty but also of possibilities. It is this that makes it perfect for expression through dance and/or music and, of course, as a perfect destination of classroom drama. Consider the stories that include a wood as a key setting. What events happen here and what sorts of characters do they involve? What specific transformation occurs in each story and what might be the most appropriate music to represent this? An evocation of the wood itself through sound would encourage children to move deeper into the setting, explore amongst the trees, touch the emotions of the characters they meet, confront their fears and press on towards the light. Of course the music chosen or composed for the wood in Little Red Riding Hood may not be appropriate for the wood in Hansel and Gretel.

Dance – This setting, a place of potential and possibility and one that is familiar, particularly in relation to fairy tales, can be used to stimulate a consideration of mood and atmosphere. The development of a potential plot through creating, adapting and linking dance actions to communicate narrative and associated emotions could also be examined.

Setting – mood and atmosphere

Moving through the wood in a range of travelling, swinging and circling movements and turns, straight and curved pathways and the use of different floor shapes could be selected as the children meander in and out of imaginary trees. The children could engage in 'follow the leader' activities, changing speeds, levels, use of body parts and the flow of the piece. *The Tunnel* by Anthony Browne is a helpful resource here. Feeling the shape and depth of a tunnel using hands, feet or elbows, for example, could set the context for this piece. The imaginary tunnel could begin small and narrow, then become large and wide, the children could journey along the tunnel by feeling the way, reaching, changing body shapes and ways of moving. Creeping, pushing, pulling, wriggling, rolling, crawling, squeezing and sliding movements could be developed. Partner work could be incorporated, or the creation of a tunnel as a group, or even as a class could be investigated. Children could move in, out, over, under and through the human tunnel by contrasting light and quick movements with slow undulating ones.

Lost in the wood – Connecting with previous work on moving through the wood and the tunnel, children's emotional responses could be conveyed, in the creation of sequences of movement incorporating exploring the surrounding space, searching high and low, hiding behind trees and moments of stillness. A phrase that incorporates slowly moving backwards then bumping into a partner, freezing, jumping then slowly turning to face each other could be added.

Process and product

Active engagement with musical and physical literacies and the compositional processes of exploration, decision-making, rehearsal and performance, motivate, energise and enable children to use their imagination, creative thinking and develop artistically. Such opportunities for creation require an understanding of the need to make connections between other texts and experience, to empathise, to consider the use of imagery and to infer and determine meaning.

References

Anholt, L. and Robbins, A. (1998) *Little Red Riding Wolf.* London: Orchard.

Browne, A. (1989) *The Tunnel.* London: Walker Books.

French, F. (1986) *Snow White in New York.* Oxford: Oxford University Press.

Hutchins, P. (1968) *Rosie's Walk.* London: The Bodley Head.

Policastro, E. and Gardner, H. (1999) 'Case studies to robust generalisations' in Sternberg, R. J. (ed.) *Handbook of Creativity.* Cambridge: Cambridge University Press.

Post, J. and Hohmann, M. (2000) *Tender Care and Early Learning Supporting Families and Toddlers in Childcare Settings.* Michigan: High/Scope Press.

Slade, P. (1954) *Child Drama.* London: University of London Press.

Chapter 13

Looking to be literate

Prue Goodwin

Seeing comes before words. The child looks and recognises before it can speak.

(Berger 1972: 7)

It took me 50 years to acknowledge the dominance of my visual mode of cognition. When I think, words are expressed through pictures in my mind, when I take notes in a lecture, I draw, and when I memorise anything – from a set of directions to someone's name – it is easiest if I create internal images around the information. On reading the opening pages of a novel my mind fills with a developing picture. It is almost like watching a film which I mentally step into at the point at which I become 'lost in the book'. These visual experiences – especially the construction of internal image when reading – are common, and visual intelligence (Gardner 1983) is recognised, and catered for, within multisensory approaches to teaching, but neither drawing nor reading pictures hold much status in schools outside the art curriculum. As with print literacy, visual literacy involves making meaning either by interpretation (reading) or through creation (representation). Children need experience of both as means of establishing cognition when encountering new ideas. This chapter considers some of the practical ways in which internal imaging and image creation has been, and can be, used by teachers to enhance the development of literacy. The chapter will look briefly at:

- reading pictures
- drawing to make meaning
- drawing to express response and understanding
- art as inspiration for writing
- the influence of the moving image.

Reading pictures

We are surrounded by visual image – so much so that we take images for granted and we are not always conscious of how an image is being used, or how our meaning-making processes are being controlled by the creators of the image. For instance, think of this picture. A piece of purple silk material is being cut by very large, sharp scissors. What does it mean? The picture appeared on a large advertising hoarding beside a busy road. Underneath the picture is some writing saying 'Smoking can kill'. Straight away many people will identify the image as an advertisement for cigarettes – some even to being able to name the brand. The poster described is one in a series for an advertising campaign that has run for several years. What part did the writing play in creating meaning? If you had not been sure about the picture, the caption underneath told you what was being promoted. It is, however, the obscure image that promotes smoking so successfully. The words are attempting to persuade you not to smoke. It has been a successful advertising campaign so it follows that the meanings associated with image are powerful – in this case, more powerful than the words.

The example above involving scissors cutting purple silk material is from an advertising campaign. What has the use of that image got to do with pictures in children's books? In common with most powerful images, such as those in advertising, pictures in books are often dismissed as purely decorative – or as something to be abandoned by readers as skill at understanding print increases. Such opinions fail to take into account that pictures, like words, express meanings which need to be interpreted if they are to be understood. Picture books that have no written text, for example, far from being easy to comprehend, can be very challenging to readers of all ages and experience. Look, for instance, at the opening pages of *Clown* by Quentin Blake. On page one we see a lady putting a clutch of toys into a dustbin. One of the toys is an expressionless clown. On the next double page spread there are nine separate images showing the clown's escape from the bin (see Figure 13.1).

In each drawing the clown's expression changes, registering his thoughts – 'I've got to get out of here!' – and his feelings – despair, concern, hope, anxiety, triumph. Turn another page and we are into a narrative that takes us through events which are in turn comic, sad, frightening and uplifting. The pages may be without print, but the general knowledge and linguistic competence required to tell the story go far beyond the levels of vocabulary usually associated with books for little children. Learning to look closely – beyond and between the line, shape, colour and space in a picture – is an essential aspect of reading visual texts, just as reading beyond the literal is essential when reading print. Good picture books provide a quality of visual text which requires sophisticated meaning making to take place. When children are encouraged to look closely, to talk about and to interpret images, they enhance their skills as critical readers (see Chapter 6 'Creativity and picture books' by Judith Graham). In their research into children's understanding of picture books, Arizpe and Styles (2003: 125) found that:

FIGURE 13.1 The clown's escape from the bin (from *Clown* by Quentin Blake, published by Jonathan Cape)

> The children . . . reveal an ability to put themselves in the artist's head to imagine how he wanted the reader to react by creating images that inspired humour, fear and other emotions. The children are also able to go inside their own heads to describe what they are thinking and feeling as they read a picture (and also as they draw one themselves). The children's critical comments and observations suggest how their metacognitive skills can be developed and built on in order to help them become more critical and discerning readers.

Learning how to read a picture goes further than an appreciation of an artist's skill or enjoyment of something pleasurable to look at. The ability to be visually critical and discriminating in our image-rich society ensures that we are not vulnerable to any visually manipulative media.

Drawing to make meaning

Just as looking at images can be demanding on cognitive processes so creating images will add an extra dimension to thinking by helping us to see – both physically and metaphorically. The Campaign for Drawing recognises that when we draw we don't just represent what we see, we demonstrate our understanding of the world. 'Ruskin saw drawing as the foundation of visual thought. His mission was not to teach people how to draw, but how to see' (www.drawingpower.org.uk). Drawings and sketches made as people think, talk, plan or listen are a means of 'thinking aloud on paper' (Hickling 2003). Representing our cognition of the world begins very early in life – as soon as an infant can wield a mark making tool.

The beginnings of writing

Drawing has long been recognised and valued as part of 'The pre-history of written language' (Vygotsky 1978) and more recent research has reinforced and developed this knowledge (Dyson 1989; Kress 1997; Styles and Bearne 2003). However, Barrs (1988), whilst fully acknowledging the evolutionary path from drawing to writing, makes the point that, when expressing meaning on paper, drawing is sometimes a far better means of representation than print:

> Drawing is certainly a better medium for representing certain meanings, and it may be helpful to consider what it is that some children can do through drawing that cannot be done through writing – what it is that they are obliged to give up or do without when they write rather than draw.
>
> First, certain kinds of description and analysis are obviously better done through drawing and diagramming than through words. Drawing can show how things work much more efficiently than writing can – engineers, architects and designers use drawing to convey their thinking. (Barrs 1988: 63)

It is not only the 'engineers, architects and designers' that find drawing the best way to record and convey their thoughts. Some writers draw before committing their ideas to print. The author Robin Jarvis, for example, has whole books from his Deptford Mice series in graphic novel form which were never intended for publication but purely as the first drafts of his novels. For many children, it is beneficial to their development as writers to offer the opportunity to draw in preparation for writing – and not just when they are in the early years of schooling. For some young writers, time given for planning a story can be most profitably spent by making sketches. The sketches will not necessarily be in any particular order. Although some may prefer the sequence of a storyboard, others may just like to 'play' with a pencil, doing doodles as a means of generating and retaining ideas.

Drawing to express response and understanding

Drawing in response to a story or poem is sometimes perceived as an 'easy' way to get children to express their ideas but such a description is undeserved. Offering children the chance to draw in response to what they have read or have had read to them provides a 'text' which can reveal the depth of their understanding more accurately than written language and which can then scaffold any spoken or written response. Take, as examples, the following occasions when children used drawing as the means to extend and express what they had understood in a story and a poem.

Drawing thinking

Children in a Year 2 class listened to a traditional tale that involved three princes who had been asked to fulfil a task by their dying father. 'Fill my room with something to make me feel better,' demanded the king. The two older sons could only come up with concrete ideas and they tried to fill the room with gold and with feathers. The youngest son spent more time thinking. He filled the room with music and laughter. The children were asked to draw the 'thinking' done by the youngest prince. There was no hesitation, no protests that they couldn't draw. Every child produced a picture that demonstrated the depth of their understanding of the story. Drawing, with the addition of a few words, musical notation and symbols (such as, thought bubbles), enabled even the least linguistically confident to express the abstract nature of thought, music and laughter. Drawing provided the means through which to demonstrate that they had penetrated the heart of the story.

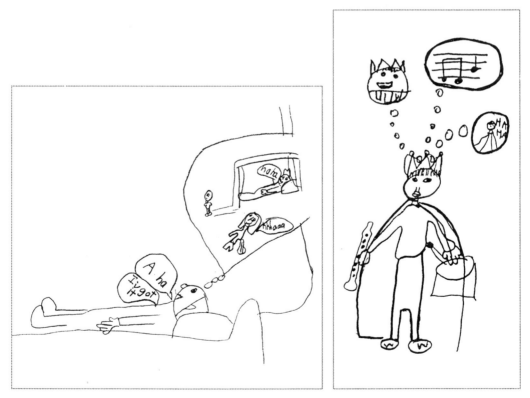

FIGURE 13.2 and 13.3 Drawings about the young prince's thinking

Drawing freedom

A similar task was set in a Year 5/6 class after reading and discussing the poem 'The Jaguar' by Ted Hughes (in Alvarez 1962). The lesson began with look at Anthony Browne's picture book *Zoo*, which raises issues about animals in captivity. Discussion about pictures from Browne's book prompted thoughts that were reflected in the poem – the idleness and apathy of the creatures, the general air of distress. The contrast of the imprisoned jaguar, lost in his own internalised world of freedom, was abstruse – an abstract concept of liberty which was difficult for the children to find words to express. Being offered the chance to draw, however, enabled them to demonstrate how well they had understood Hughes' words. The session finished with a look at Helen Cowcher's picture book *Jaguar* which gave a further reflection on the life of the caged animal. It is worthwhile allowing time in school to develop pupils' visual literacy as a means of demonstrating understanding or as a vehicle to help free the complex meanings encountered within the written word.

FIGURE 13.4 and 13.5 Drawings about the poem 'The Jaguar' by Ted Hughes

Art as inspiration for writing

Writing can engender an artistic response and, equally, art work can inspire a written response. Teachers have harnessed the power of great artists to motivate young writers for many years. The following examples of art-based projects show the children's facility to link the visual with the literary.

FIGURE 13.6 and 13.7 Drawings about the poem 'The Jaguar' by Ted Hughes

'Tell Me a Picture'

As part of his two-year role as Children's Laureate, Quentin Blake was instrumental in setting up an exhibition at the National Gallery entitled 'Tell me a picture'. An 'alphabet' of artists was exhibited whose paintings had in common the potential for generating great stories. At the gallery itself, viewers were invited to create stories around each picture. The pictures also appeared on the National Gallery website where children were invited to write in response to each picture. Finished stories were emailed back to the gallery education staff who put selected stories on the website for all to read. An important part of the experience was to validate children's interpretations of and imaginative responses to each painting. The simple concept behind Blake's exhibition can be replicated in any classroom – even to the extent of creating an interactive task on the computer. Teachers can find works of art to hand in local art galleries or through a picture loan service (make enquiries at the local library or education authority). There are also many books full of wonderful pictures, including the catalogue of the 'Tell me a picture' exhibition (Blake 2001).

The Visual Paths Project

The Visual Paths Project, run by Colin Grigg at the Tate Modern and Tate Britain galleries in London, confirmed and extended awareness of the power of art to inspire (Grigg

2003a). The Visual Paths Project connected children, writers, actors and illustrators with works of art in order to explore the interaction between text and image. Children were invited to write in response to the works of art to which they had been introduced. The intention was that children would write whatever they wished, whatever the artwork moved them to say. Grigg explained: 'The children's responses do not attempt to translate the artworks into words, but read in relation to the artworks they bring new depths of interpretation which enhance and deepen understanding' (Grigg 2003b: 134)

As a result of the Visual Paths Project, renowned picture book author/artist Anthony Browne, one of the authors involved, produced a picture book which encapsulates the way artwork can fascinate, motivate and inspire. *The Shape Game* (Browne 2003) illustrates the transforming power of art and its power to lead to creative response. The book itself can act as inspiration for teachers and learners to effect further writing, art work, gallery visits, etc.

The book arts

Paul Johnson's work on the book arts (Johnson 1990, 1993) illustrates the ways in which different forms of presentation can motivate children to write.

> When children plan and design a book of their own, integrate handwriting, lettering, illustration, and binding as a vehicle for the communication of ideas, a superior kind of mental activity comes into play.   (Johnson 1993: 14)

Johnson's approach is strongly advocated by the Institute of Education at the University of Reading. Following a course with lecturer, Heather Leonard, trainee teachers are encouraged to reflect on the impact of book making on their pupils. Lucy Mewton, a trainee teacher reflecting on book making as part of her school experience, wrote: 'Children who normally struggled or felt intimidated by a blank page relished the different presentation and actually focused their thinking and completed work. One very inattentive child who rarely finished work produced the best work yet – finishing and improving, as well as illustrating, his work' (extract from an evaluation of a literacy lesson; unpublished 2003).

The influence of the moving image

The days are long gone when experienced teachers saw television or film as bad influences on young readers and writers. Being at ease with multimedia texts is the norm for pupils, and teachers benefit from harnessing children's experience of computer, TV and film texts as they learn to read and write. Some indication of how much children's visual experiences influence their thinking when writing was provided by group of confident young writers from Year 5. The following extracts from the discussion on writing stories illustrate the influence of moving image.

Helen: When my teacher gives me the title of a story I always think and then I actually picture the story so that I can remember – then you can do it bit by bit. And the picture's in my head.

Ben: You have a picture in your head and you're just like printing it out.

Chris: Sort of like a film in your head.

The children readily described their internal imaging as 'like a film' although the use of storyboards or sketching when planning for writing was unfamiliar to them. It is evident that they continued to be conscious of returning to mental images as the ongoing process of composition was taking place.

Helen: It's like reading a book to yourself reading in sections like chapters... um... you read one chapter then you stop and... well you stop and put the book down and it's like you're putting writing on a piece of paper and then you have to stop and think what's the rest of the picture that's in your mind. And then you write it down again and keep on doing it from there.

Oliver: My pen's doing the writing I have to look down sometimes to make sure I'm writing on the line. In my mind's eye I see the page... the picture behind it, behind the writing.

PG: So you've got the writing but you've also got the image...?

Oliver: Yeah, but I'm not looking at the writing. It's not focused, if you know what I mean.

Oliver described two sorts of thinking working simultaneously. He was conscious of writing on the page at the same time as being aware of a 'film' running through his head. Many of the more traditional plans for story writing fail to take into account that, for some children, experience of visual texts, internal imaging and external sketching of ideas may be of more value than written notes about setting or character. Some of the most powerful stories that children know are those they have watched. It follows that some of the most powerful pieces of writing they encounter are the scripts of TV dramas and films. The combination of word and image has been a natural part of the multimedia-rich world all youngsters have grown up in. It makes sense to make the most of pupils' visual and graphic skills in the classroom when it comes to the complex task of writing.

Conclusion

The pictures in our minds are important. The drawings we scribble onto paper are expressions of ideas, thoughts and feelings. When tackling the complexities of the literacy curriculum, allowing children to visualise and to draw is of benefit to all. For some learners, not to let them use their visual abilities will seriously disadvantage them. And it isn't just literacy learning that gains from children being free to draw;

study of every subject, especially those that require problem-solving, will be enhanced.

Acknowledgements

Thanks to the children of schools in Berkshire and Surrey: Onslow Infants, Queen Eleanor's Juniors, Sandfield Primary and Aldermaston Primary.

References

Alvarez, A. (1962) *The new poetry*. London: Penguin.

Arizpe, E. and Styles, M. (2003) 'Picture book and metaliteracy: How children describe the processes of creation and reception' in Styles, M. and Bearne, E. (1988) *Art, narrative and childhood*, pp. 115–25. Stoke-on-Trent: Trentham Books.

Barrs, M. (1988) 'Drawing a story: Transitions between drawing and writing', in Lightfoot, M. and Martin, N. *The word for teaching is learning*, pp. 51–69. London: Heinemann Educational Books.

Berger, J. (1972) *Ways of seeing*. London: Penguin.

Blake, Q. (1995) *Clown*. London: Jonathan Cape.

Blake, Q. (2001) *Tell me a picture*. London: National Gallery Company Limited.

Browne, A. (1992) *Zoo*. London: Julia MacRae Books.

Browne, A. (2003) *The Shape Game*. London: Doubleday.

Cowcher, H. (1997) *Jaguar*. London: Scholastic Children's Books.

Dyson, A. H. (1989) *Multiple worlds of child writers: Friends learn to write*. New York: Columbia University Teachers College Press.

Gardner, H. (1983) *Frames of mind: The theory of multiple intelligences*. London: Heinemann.

Grigg, C. (ed.) (2003a) *Visual Paths to Literacy: A handbook for Gallery Educators and Teachers*. London: Tate National Programmes.

Grigg, C. (2003b) 'The painted word: Literacy through art' in Styles, M. and Bearne, E. (eds) *Art, narrative and childhood*, pp. 127–36. Stoke-on-Trent: Trentham Books.

Hickling, A. (2003) 'The stage of drawing', critique of a Tate Liverpool exhibition, *The Guardian*, 13 October.

Johnson, P. (1990) *A book of one's own*. London: Hodder & Stoughton.

Johnson, P. (1993) *Literacy through the book arts*. London: Hodder & Stoughton.

Kress, G. (1997) *Before writing: Rethinking paths to literacy*. London: Routledge.

Styles, M. and Bearne, E. (eds) (2003) *Art, narrative and childhood*. Stoke-on-Trent: Trentham Books.

Vygotsky, L. S. (1978) *Mind in society*. Cambridge, Mass.: Harvard University Press.

Chapter 14

Literacy, creativity and moving image media

Wendy Earle

I have been more surprised by the children's reactions to the films than anything else I have ever seen. (Year 5 teacher involved in BFI pilot project for *Story Shorts*)

Helping children to improve their ability to infer meaning from a text is an issue for every tired pre-SATs teacher in the land; and yet here were Y3 children showing how easy it can be. We were amazed.

(Joe Brian reviewing *Story Shorts*, *The Primary English Magazine*, June 2002)

While being able to read and write is the basic requirement for literacy, it is not a sufficient one. Literacy is – or at least should be – far more than this. The National Literacy Strategy (NLS) is now well bedded into primary schools, however, every year when test results are published, the same discussion arises about whether the approaches to literacy teaching are too narrow, and whether pupils get enough scope to explore and reflect on texts in greater depth and to create their own, and how this affects standards. The recent emphasis on creativity is, perhaps, an attempt to redress this by encouraging teachers to explore ways of engaging children's minds more actively in their schoolwork. However, given the extent of confusion around what creativity actually means, this is not an unproblematic process.

The linked issues of literacy, creativity and moving image media are a core concern of *BFI* Education at the British Film Institute. Among other things, we have been looking at how moving image media can be used to support literacy teaching and have been involved in an evaluation of a pilot project by Becta to promote creativity through digital video technology. In this chapter I want to put the case for integrating moving image media (film, video and television) into the literacy curriculum. In order to do this I first need to identify some of the issues relating to literacy and creativity, which informs the case for using moving image media more extensively in teaching. I will then look at some examples of how the use of moving image media and technology can enhance literacy.

Essentially, the development of literacy in children is about the development of their minds – their capacity for thought. While being literate is necessary to being a fully informed citizen, to participate in society, it is also about the development of the individual as an independent thinking human being. Ideally this means an individual who can think beyond immediate concerns and preoccupations and take in the 'bigger picture'.

Learning how to think

Margaret Donaldson suggests, in her seminal work, *Children's Minds* (1978), that the main objective of education is to enable children to learn how to think in ways that don't necessarily make 'human sense'. Things that easily make sense to us tend to be rooted in our experience and knowledge of how things happen in the real world. Children come to school with well-established skills as thinkers but their thinking is directed 'outwards on the real, meaningful, shifting, distracting world'. Young children tend to mix up the relationship between cause and effect and not fully grasp logical links and consequences. In order to succeed at school children need to be able to 'direct their own thought processes in a thoughtful manner' and to do this they must be able to manipulate symbols – 'not just talk but choose what they want to say, not just interpret but weigh possible interpretations'.

The necessary basis for this is an awareness of language as a symbol system – an awareness that cannot be assumed when children start school. The process of learning to read is closely entwined with the development of children's consciousness of words as symbols separate from what they represent. While children need to have some sense of this in order to be ready to learn to read, in learning to read and write they deepen their grasp of the symbol system and how it works to convey meaning. Whereas children learn to speak unconsciously, in learning to read, and even more so in learning to write, they become conscious of language as an abstraction from reality, not reality itself. Ideally they learn to interpret, appreciate and evaluate meaning. They learn that texts are constructed, and that they represent not just things they can see and touch, but ideas and thoughts that aren't physical and concrete. Simultaneously children gradually acquire self-awareness – they become conscious of their own thought, and this awareness is essential to the development of children's ability to grasp difficult concepts, and to develop and manipulate their own ideas. 'If children are going to control and direct their own thinking, . . . they must become conscious of it' (Donaldson, p. 94).

It could be argued that this self-controlling and directing of thought is the basis of the creative process. As children begin to grasp the way texts are constructed they can also learn how to work within and (probably later) subvert these codes to express their own ideas. Creativity, as defined by the National Advisory Committee on Creative and Cultural Education (NACCCE) and the Qualifications and Curriculum Authority (QCA), is 'imaginative activity in pursuit of a defined purpose, or goals, ending in the production of something original, which has value for the maker' (NACCCE 1999).

This definition is somewhat problematic. As pointed out in the Becta Digital Video pilot (see Reid *et al.* 2002), originality is not sufficient because something could be original without being meaningful. And, besides, how is it decided that something is original? Most creative work emerges out of a process of learning and thinking about existing texts, ideas, concepts and reality, and creative products are often the result of a problem-solving process within a set of specific constraints. Reid *et al.*, in their report, noted that where teachers understood creativity as freedom from constraint, and played no clear role in preparing children for creative activity, the resulting videos were far less effective. (See pages 25–26 and 75–77, *BFI* Evaluation Report for discussion of these issues.) Creativity essentially involves self-directed, self-controlled thinking, using existing knowledge and understanding to create something new. Creating a new text involves choosing both what you want to say and how you want to say it.

Moving image media and children's thought

What role can moving image media play in the development of children's thought – their ability to read and interpret texts, to reflect on and shape their own thinking, and to create their own meaningful texts? First of all we should recognise that moving image media, while not strictly speaking symbol systems as such, do involve signification. They do not simply record or reflect reality: they represent and shape it on the screen through a range of codes and conventions.

If we accept that literacy is more than just decoding text, that it involves interpreting and reflecting on the meanings of the text, and creating new texts, then there is scope for similar kinds of thinking work to be done in relation to moving image texts. On the whole visual representations of reality are more readily perceivable, easier to make sense of to viewers, however young or inexperienced. However, to grasp their intended meanings, particularly at a more complex or subtle level, requires an understanding of the codes and conventions that govern this form of communication. Just as print texts have grammatical codes that help to structure them, knowledge of which helps the reader interpret them, so moving image texts have codes and conventions that give them shape and meaning.

Paul Messaris (1994: 135), in his illuminating discussion of visual literacy, argues that visually literate viewers are, to some degree at least, 'self-conscious of their role as interpreters', and they have some 'explicit awareness about the processes by which meaning is created through the visual media'. He suggests that this awareness does not arise naturally, out of the process of viewing, but is based on formal learning about the components of film-making. A visually literate viewer starts from the understanding that 'a particular image, feature of an image, or juxtaposition of images should be taken as a deliberate expression of an intended meaning'.

Visual literacy (or cine-literacy, as it has been defined more specifically in relation to moving images) involves an understanding of the conventions and codes of films, but also requires some knowledge, according to Messaris and others, of film production and film traditions. As defined in *Making Movies Matter*, the BFI's report on moving image education in the UK,

> A cineliterate person has a knowledge of the history, contemporary range and social context of moving images, the ability to analyse and explain how moving image media make meaning and achieve effects, and some skill in the production of moving image media. (1999)

The stages through which this knowledge and understanding can be introduced are suggested in the bfi's learning progression model 'Becoming Cineliterate' in *Moving Images in the Classroom* (2000), which can be matched against the English National Curriculum Key Stages 1 and up.

Visual literacy

In recent years, many arguments have been made for recognising and promoting visual literacy. Two main strands of these arguments are that it enables teachers to use pupils' cultural knowledge as a way of engaging them in the literacy process, and that it acts as a bridge to print literacy. However, another argument that seems to be less well recognised outside the media education lobby, is that cine-literacy provides children with tools for analysing and interpreting, at a deeper level, media which take up many of their leisure hours and influence their perceptions of the world in which they live. Therefore, as David Buckingham and others have pointed out, children come to school already with a high level of existing knowledge about the media. Teachers can 'enable students to build upon this knowledge, to develop new insights and understandings' (Buckingham 1990).

Buckingham refers to Vygotsky's exposition on the development of 'scientific concepts', which are scientific in the sense of being characterised by a distance from lived experience, and of involving both an ability to generalise in a systematic way and self-reflection – a self-conscious attention to the thought process. Through the learning of scientific concepts students can begin to integrate spontaneous concepts – knowledge and understandings they have but are not necessarily conscious of having – into a system. Given children's enormous experience of moving image media texts, they can often talk about these texts knowledgeably. However, if cine-literacy were part of the school curriculum, children's understanding of these texts, and their ability to talk and write about them, could be significantly enhanced. As Buckingham (1990) puts it:

> The aim of media education, then, is not merely to enable children to 'read' – or make sense of – media texts, or to enable them to 'write' their own: it must also enable them to reflect systematically on the process of reading and writing themselves, to understand and to analyse their own activity as readers and writers.

Story Shorts

In developing *Story Shorts* – a video compilation of short films for use in the literacy hour at Key Stage 2 – colleagues in *BFI* Education demonstrated the potential for short films in using children's familiarity with moving image media to enhance their understanding of both film and print texts, as well as to develop their writing. When teachers use moving image texts in the classroom they often rely on what children are already familiar with, partly because they see this familiarity as a positive way of endorsing children's cultural experience and partly because these texts are easily available. We wanted to use texts that might challenge expectations and extend children's experience of moving image media. We selected five films, from three minutes to 14 minutes long, that represent a range of filmic and narrative styles. Four of them are animations and one is live action; two of them include dialogue, two use only music and one has just natural sound effects; three of them are narratives with a 'beginning, middle and end' and two of them are more abstract and impressionistic.

We wanted to show how making children aware of some of the conventions of film construction could enhance their literacy skills. As David Parker (2002: 40) has written:

> The responses of the consultants and teachers who have used *Story Shorts* over an extended period back up our developing hypothesis that there are deep links between narrative structures across print and moving image media which can be used to support writing development. There is, in a sense, a scaffolding effect taking place when ... films are used by teachers as texts to be read by children in detailed ways.

One of the consultants working on the *Story Shorts* pilot, Collette Higgins (2002: 30), has detailed how –

> All pupils quickly tuned into the concept of camera angle for highlighting main events or small details in the visual text. They absorbed the technical terms of 'camera angle', 'long shot', 'mid-shot' and 'close up', 'panning' and 'tilting' into their vocabulary and, towards the end of the week, most were able to apply the parallels in their writing:

Drawing the reader's eye upwards:

The church bells high up in the tower, ringing loudly introduced a new day.

The birds were flying in perfect formation over the church.

Drawing the reader's eye down:

It snatched the pole from his hand and it plummeted to the bottom of the gorge.

Drawing attention to small detail:

His cloak was tied at the top with a golden brooch in the shape of a medallion.

In the centre was a silver balancing pole and under it was an engraving that said 'El Caminante'.

Higgins offers many more examples of the powerful impact of studying this film, *El Caminante*, on the writing by this group of boys. They watched the film several times during the week, with the teacher using it to explore setting, narrative structure, beginnings and endings, the creation of tension and character development. As demonstrated by the above extracts, the boys' writing was enriched by the process and reports from their teacher indicated a more self-conscious approach to crafting their writing for specific effect.

Making videos, including live action and animated films, offers children another way of consciously shaping their texts. Increasingly low cost digital video technology has made it more possible than ever before for schools to give their children access to it. Digital video editing, in particular, offers a real breakthrough in the possibilities for constructing moving image texts in school.

Effective film-making is a lot more than pointing a camera and shooting. This might create a record of events, but it does little else. Making a film requires planning and forethought. Film-makers, like authors, need to consider what they want to say and how they want to say it; but they also need to draw together a range of elements – visual, aural and written – which requires co-ordination and organisation. There are opportunities for writing, such as in preparing a 'pitch' for their film and creating a screenplay. Storyboarding requires pupils to think about how they want to build to a climax, what detail they want to focus on, how sound and image relate, etc. The editing process involves children in thinking about how the material they have shot could be constructed together (whether their original storyboard works, or whether they want to modify the structure), and in experimenting on how different types and juxtapositions of shots can change meanings.

As David Parker (2003: 43) has pointed out in reporting research on an animation project in Dundee primary schools:

> The use of script and storyboard workshops by the writer-in-residence reframes the act of writing so that its end purpose is filmic and this draws on important aspects of children's knowledge of media texts.

In addition, the process of experimenting with the construction of video texts has huge potential for helping children to grasp the different ways that meaning is made and how they can develop and present connections (such as cause and effect) between events in a narrative.

However, it should not be taken for granted that children's familiarity with media texts spontaneously translates into creative activity with digital video technology. In their evaluation of the Becta Digital Video Pilot in primary and secondary schools, Mark Reid *et al.* (2002) reported that poor quality work often resulted from an unthinking, spontaneous and unstructured use of the technology. In contrast, when teachers harnessed children's familiarity of moving image media and made sure they had a conscious 'understanding and an appreciation of the language of the moving image', children produced effective and successful videos. Successful work included 'the creation of stylistic features such as humour, irony and genre pastiche', coherent and imaginative visual composition, thoughtful and effective use of lighting and sound, coherent sequencing and transitions of shots, and purposeful use of rhythm. All of these features required children to take a conscious and systematic approach to their work. They needed to think at a number of levels about how different elements of their films would work together, and they also needed to constantly stand back and consider whether the film was achieving the desired effect, creating the intended meanings.

In the mid-1980s, Neil Postman alerted us to the problem that children's exposure to media texts was changing their way of thinking. He argued that a different kind of learning took place through television and electronic media than through print. Whereas through learning to read and write, children learned to distance themselves from immediate experience, to assess and evaluate information and ideas, electronic media (specifically television) tends to develop in children an impressionistic, superficial attitude to knowledge and information. However, he didn't see this as an inevitable process if educators took on the task of assisting children to 'learn how to distance themselves from their forms of information' (Postman 1987). Connecting literacy, creativity and moving image media is surely one way of helping children achieve this distance. If children have the necessary tools of analysis, can 'not just talk but choose what [they want] to say, not just interpret but weigh possible interpretations' in relation to moving image texts, and have opportunities to create increasingly complex texts of their own, the potential is for electronic media to enhance rather than undermine education.

References

Buckingham, D. (1990) 'Making it Explicit: Towards a Theory of Media Learning' in Buckingham, D. (ed.) (1990) *Watching Media Learning*, pp. 215–28. London: Falmer Press.

British Film Institute (2000) *Moving Images in the Classroom*. London: British Film Institute.

Donaldson, M. (1978) *Children's Minds*. London: Penguin Books.

Higgins, C. (2002) 'Using Film Texts to Support Reluctant Writers', *English in Education*, 36 (1), 25–37.

Messaris, P. (1994) *Visual Literacy: Image, Mind and Reality*. Oxford: Westview.

Parker, D. (2002) 'Show Us A Story: An Overview of Recent Research and Resource Development Work at the British Film Institute', *English in Education,* 36 (1), 38–45.

Postman, N. (1987) *Amusing Ourselves to Death*. London: Methuen.

Reid, M., Parker, D. and Burn, A. (2002) Evaluation Report of the Becta Digital Video Project, http://www.becta.org.uk/research/reports/digitalvideo/

Index

Printed in the United Kingdom
by Lightning Source UK Ltd.
126064UK00005B/8/A